Photography and Schizophrenia

Acknowledgements

To my parents, Ed and Florence Manthei, for caring about me and believing in me when I had no hope at times.

I owe some real gratitude to Trudy Dawson, my therapist, who wrote the forward to this book and who has worked with me since 1998 helping me maintain stability and helping me to put my life back together.

And this is also to acknowledge the therapists and psychiatrists who have worked with me going back to 1963 and who intervened before it was too late and prevented me from ending my life in the darker periods of my existence.

And to myself for staying on my meds and staying in treatment and not giving up—for choosing responsibility and integrity and the courage to live and face life in all its light and darkness. And for the years I was on disability which kept me from falling through the cracks--where I learned the value of a dollar and that mental health comes with incredible discipline and a lot of emotional work and is not without some rewards and satisfactions when you hang in there.

For my friends who respected me and believed in me and cared and who did not judge me.

I have a great respect and appreciation for the people who have been in my life who have been honest, caring, and responsible.
So, with this I pay it forward to other people who might just be starting out on their journeys and others who have known unspeakable pain and are trying to do things the right way.

Photography & Schizophrenia

By

Jean Marie Manthei, MA, LPC, CAS

[a schizophrenic counselor's interpretation of this]
Forward by Trudy Dawson, LCSW
Author and photographer Jean Manthei
and
early childhood photographs
by Ed Manthei, Jean's father,
and Les Roberts
A few pictures are taken of Jean by other
students when Jean was in school.

Copyright 2023 by Jean-Marie Manthei, MA, LPC, CAS
All rights reserved.

No part of this book may be reproduced or transmitted in any form or by any means, graphic, electronic, or mechanical, including photocopying, recording, taping or by any information storage retrieval system, without the permission in writing, from Jean Manthei or the publisher.

This book is non-fiction.

TRUDY C. DAWSON, MSW, LCSW, PC
Licensed Clinical Social Worker
Psychotherapy, Consultation, Training and Hypnotherapy

February 2, 2023

RE: Foreward to ***Photography and Schizophrenia***

I have known Jean Manthei, both as her therapist and colleague, since 1998. To work with a patient, such as Jean, who has the diagnosis of Schizophrenia, yet is high functioning as a Licensed Professional Counselor and Certified Addictions specialist, has been both challenging and rewarding. My work with Jean has given me the unique experience and privilege of enlightenment and awareness of the extreme difficulties of living with Schizophrenia, through Jean's eyes. This photo book, likewise, will give others an opportunity to gain that same privilege and enlightenment, through Jean's camera lens.

Jean has successfully managed to live and cope with Schizophrenia, along with significant life traumas and losses. As a therapist, she has been a tireless advocate in helping others overcome their addictions. As an author and writer, she continues in this pursuit by sharing her own story through photographs. This book captures that philosophy of resiliency, the ability to overcome adversity despite challenges in life. It is more than a photo book, it is a road map that provides a path that others can follow in overcoming difficult times.

Jean is an author that is uniquely qualified to publish this book. Her book, ***Photography and Schizophrenia***, is inspirational, powerful, and life changing.

Respectfully,

Trudy C Dawson

Trudy C. Dawson, MSW, LCSW, PC
Licensed Clinical Social Worker

7035 Campus Drive, Suite 808
Colorado Springs, CO 80920
www.trudycdawson.com

Phone: 719-377-2118
Fax: 877-515-7171
Email: therapy@trudycdawson.com

Table of Contents

Acknowledgements............................. 2

Forward by Trudy Dawson, LCSW.................. 4

Chapter 1: Integrity and the Importance of Choice....... 6

Chapter 2: Sidetracked...........................109

Chapter 3: Age 10 with a Camera...................132

Chapter 4: Photography, Schizophrenia and Healing.....133

Epilogue.....................................178

Bibliography 194

Index..197

Chapter 1

Integrity and the Importance of Choice

I am in the process of choosing several Adobe Stock images that I pasted my picture of myself I had the drone take from the air to purchase from Adobe Stock with my Creative Cloud membership. I respect copyrights and to give credit where credit is due. I found the images of the chess pieces and the image of the sand dunes and the hour glass and a few others a great place to put my drone photo to illustrate some ideas, i.e. the sand dune and hour glass picture to illustrate the feelings of Covid19 isolation. And it was still worth it to me to invest $79 for the commercial license to use those particular pictures. The key here is not to go into debt getting the Adobe Stock images for my book. I just went to my first Debtor's Anonymous meeting this morning and that might be the first lesson.

In reverence for Debtor's Anonymous I decided not to use the Adobe Stock images and instead place myself flying the drone around some marigolds and in a labyrinth. In therapy it was decided that charging $475 worth of stock images which would only be 5 or 6 images for commercial license would create too much stress and that I would have to debt to do so. This was a difficult thing to do--to not act on impulse.

As a reward for not charging $475 for 6 commercial Adobe Stock images I got some marble chess pieces and put them on my scratched chess board and snapped pictures of them and put my drone picture in them. I replaced the 5 other Adobe Stock images with more of my own work--maybe not as spectacular or shiny--but then the work in this book is, except for Ed and Florence Manthei's contribution and a picture by Les Roberts, and a few by other students of me at schools I was in in high school and one by Chris Haynes, is work by my own talent. Not only was I learning a lesson this week of self-control and not debting when I really wanted to get those images, but I learned about the integrity of my own work--to present you with a book of Jean Manthei's photographs which are reflecting the talent of a schizophrenic counselor and photog; images that are good and sometimes not technically perfect, but my own. In presenting my work, the authenticity is preserved, and the reader can say that they are looking at the work of someone with schizophrenia instead of shiny things that come from Adobe Stock.

A perfect picture of the Boogie Man that haunts me with schizophrenia, PTSD, and trauma and sometimes shame and humiliation. This had to suffice. Bokeh, my dog had to be a stand in for the Boogie Man. Jaw snapping monster and Boogie Man--good job Bokeh!

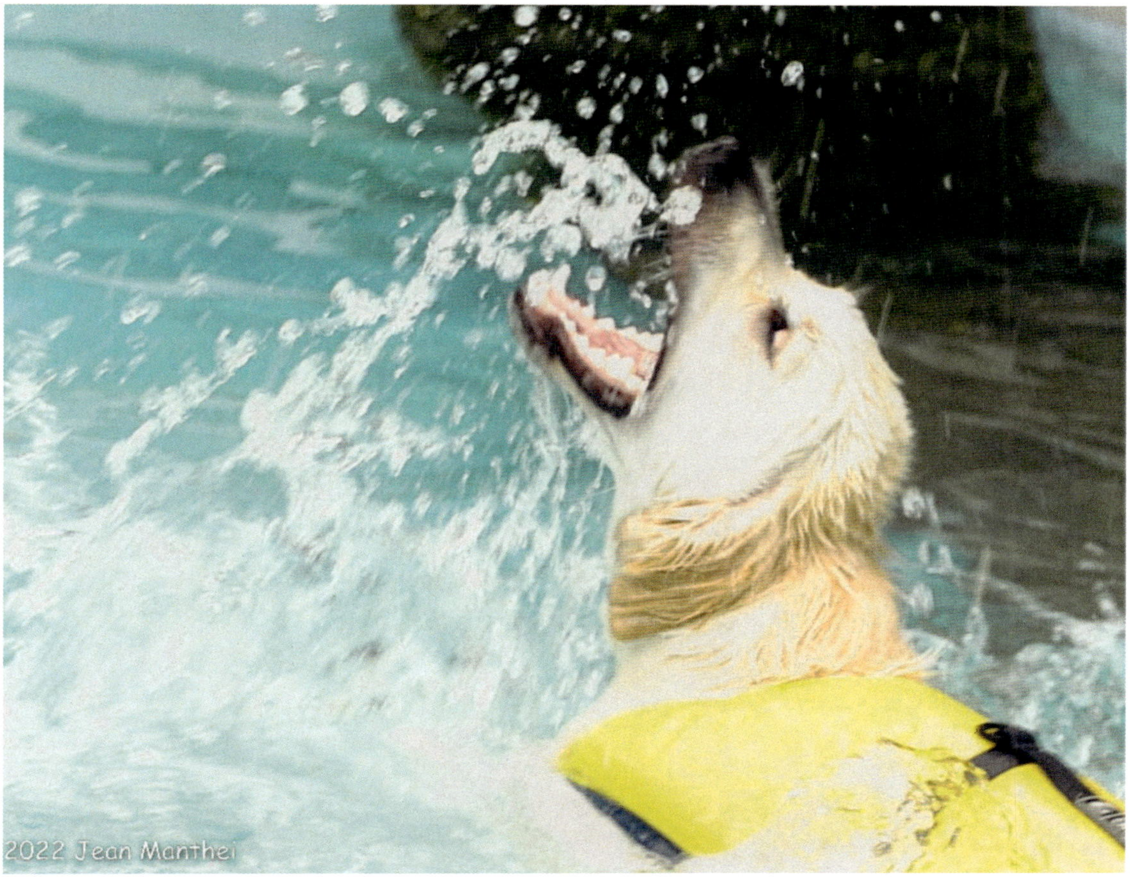
2022 Jean Manthei

Covid19
Isolation

Walking the talk. The labyrinth.

The ghosts and the spirits like it when people walk the talk, do the right things, play nice and act responsible and play well with others. The ghosts really like it if
you don't hurt others or yourself and when you are creative.

The drone--Igloo which helped me overcome my fear of death to get this thing in the air and really fly it and not hit anything or crash it. The whirring sound of the propellers capture a death instinct or fear of death. It became a tool which could be used by clients in cognitive behavioral therapy for meditation and overcoming fears.

The picture I had my drone take from the air of me flying the thing. It is this picture of me I outlined and placed in several Adobe Stock images. When I decided not to use the stock images, I put it in my own images.

You win in recovery if you do not play games or hurt people; you overcome this illness by doing the right things, being creative and being rooted in gratitude instead of resentment. You win when you take responsibility and give back to society. You win when you are just yourself and can think of others. You win when you keep your humor, your integrity, and your courage. You win when you do the very best you can with what you have and don't take from others. You win when you walk the talk. It is the winning hand.

You win when you play fair and are honest with others and are in good faith. And you just pray that you don't lose your way and must compromise your integrity. You win when you have made mistakes in your life and did your best in treatment or 12 Step groups to correct them and move forward.

This was a preset by Scott Kelby of Day to Night.
This was my efforts in 2017 and 2018 to overcome my fears of death with the little drone Igloo.

Circa March 2019.

I'm sitting here in my study and there is a blizzard forming. I've got a day off work because we're closed. And I want to get my groceries picked up and my tax information dropped off and be back here before 11 when the storm hits.

I have this dread disease of schizophrenia that was diagnosed in 1979. I was on disability from 1979 to 1997 when I got off because I proved I could work. But a lot happened in between then.

I wasn't sure where I was going with this. It struck me that in all my years of illness, decades of treatment and a couple of decades of snapping photos that there might be a connection between photography and schizophrenia. Was willing to explore that.

First, I don't think there have been any studies done documenting schizophrenia and the use of photography as a therapeutic tool for rebuilding, integrating and healing fragmented thoughts and images or trauma. There are a lot of therapists in the UK that have been inspired by Judy Weiser's ideas on therapy and photography. And a lot of people are now recognizing the value of photography in working with mental disorders.

Many schizophrenics might not possess cameras and equipment to be able to snap pictures in a more organized fashion—where intellectual property and visual property is created. How many schizophrenics have computers or iMacs and 70D or 6D Canon cameras? How many of us stay in one place long enough to create a little library with wall art and photo books? How many schizophrenics could accumulate photo books? How many schizophrenics could afford to buy them and accumulate them on a regular basis to document their illness, PTSD, abuse and broken spirits or relationships?

I happen to have hording tendencies with my schizophrenia and was able to start building book, photo and journal libraries since the 1980s. I very well earned those organizing skills in high school, college and graduate school. How many schizophrenics get to go on to do college and graduate work? A lot more of us are getting degrees and becoming professionals.

Nevertheless, I developed a pile of likeable photo trash and things. I had immense fun putting all my visual creations in photo books and on wall art. It made me feel important and as though I was doing something worthwhile.

In fact, I got so many 16x20 metal prints that I made a photo gallery in my backyard and called it Jean Manthei's Snapshot Gallery: Be Inspired.

I don't much care for National Geographic photography because it is "too perfect." I really like my work—rough as it is—especially the blown out and high key images. Some of my butterfly pictures have a sort of ethereal quality to them and others are sort of fragments because of blown out areas to make it seem like there are broken fragments and missing pieces like missing parts of myself.

Aside from just liking to snap photos there is something about holding a camera and trusting your unconscious to say something intelligent related to Jung's shadow, persona, anima, animus, conscious or unconscious and dreams. There is something about trusting my unconscious to create visions that are healing and contain wholeness, magic, playfulness and humor. Holding a camera to take a landscape or selfie picture, photos of objects and trusting my unconscious to speak about things in me that are broken, ill and schizophrenic in a way creates insight, well-being and healing that has been something that has challenged me on many levels. I trust myself to find photos that respect myself and my illness and the work I did to become a counselor despite my illness as well as to author a book.

When I think about it my unconscious is intelligent and my emotions have bent over backwards all these years helping me to create something beautiful and powerful and to make statements about life, art, and illness.

Because I trusted myself and my photographic ability, I was able to write my book ***On Gratitude***. Because I listened to my emotional self and inner child, I was able to produce my masterpiece ***On Gratitude*** and the ideas for trailers and marketing the book. It didn't seem all that important that I was successful or would sell a lot of books. Gratitude in me said "You have a home to live in, food to eat, a nice dog, a couple of computers and a camera and a car, what do you need to sell a million copies of ***On Gratitude*** for?" (Maybe to help other schizophrenics or fund programs that make it possible for people with mental disorders to achieve success, go to school or publish books). I paid for the things like cameras from my work as counselor and not the sales of books.

What then about photography and schizophrenia? Could this be a new therapy tool?

This started out as an idea—everything starts out as an idea and then you say what comes to mind and if it sounds good it becomes real and then research teams come along and do studies and document everything and then your theory becomes sort of a fact. In editing I thought "who talks like that?" and I realized I had sometimes adopted Scott Kelby's style and humor as I approached the topic of photography and schizophrenia. A thanks to Mr. Kelby for his influence on me (Kelby, 2007). For now, it is a creative idea, and I will let it form as I write these pages.

I expect if hospitals had cameras and computers for clients to use which they do in the UK, and they are allowed to tell their stories in photo books that were provided for by the hospitals clients might find that to be a great healing tool.

Photography and schizophrenia could be pretentious—it could be nothing. My inner child, Igloo says "No it's not b.s." So, I'm going to listen to my inner child. Maybe Igloo has something valuable to say about photography and schizophrenia. Afterall I've been schizophrenic for decades. Probably since I picked up a Kodak Instamatic camera at Judson school when I was 15 in 1965. Then pictures were about attractive friends in your cache of pictures and doing things like looking as if you were consuming alcohol when you couldn't stand being sedated in any way or how it made you feel. Photographs were about getting cool ski pictures or pictures of your friends in the smoking corral at school or at the Concho. They were mindless photos to misrepresent yourself and your friends. These pictures helped you see that so that when you went to therapy you could say "This isn't me—I hate alcohol." "This isn't me—I'm not rich or popular or fantastic or incredible or any of that." And then you become real in your journey through the land of therapy. The photographs could read between the lines before I could—the photographs forced me to be authentic and tell the truth. Then at 16 I went to Switzerland (Suisse). My photographs then became magical. European architecture and mountains and the flavor of depth and increasing desire for authenticity as I studied all the literature of the existentialists [my folder containing my Chatelaine pictures was missing as well as the originals so I don't have them here to show what I was doing at 16 with those photos—I then did find my scrapbook so I will enter some here].

There was an increasing need for responsibility, and these hardly seemed to be the thing that would be prodromal precursors to a schizophrenic break with reality.

After I had a child out of wedlock at 17, I gave her up for adoption and I thought I had done it all and seen it all, but I was ready to once again see the world. I was still a child myself to attempt to be a parent. I still had spirit and curiosity and soul.

When I went back to Judson in 1968, I left school for a party without permission. I suppose I felt if I was old enough to have a child, I was old enough to do what I wanted to do. I was a little too old, even at 17 to still be in high school after having a child. Yet I was not.

The party off campus turned out to be a group of people who were lying in wait for me to show up with my cap gun. And they gave me some cannabis laced with something—maybe PCP. And then they stung me and tried to murder me under the influence of this drug. I was lucky to walk away from there alive. I'm sure they knew they must have done something. After I lost consciousness, they could have done anything to me. I was in a half a million dollar house where there was stockpiles of drugs and corruption. How did I end up at a party there? They were an exciting family to some of the students at Judson.

So, there was a real break with reality with an attempt on my life. A schizophrenia that was latent turned into a full-blown psychotic episode that was based in reality.

Then I ended up getting framed for marijuana seeds after I graduated from high school that winter. At this time, I am forming some real negative impressions of drugs, the drug world, corrupt law enforcement and dirty playing fields.

I ended up living with a man who was the best friend of the person that framed me for marijuana seeds. We went to San Francisco. At that point I thought I was going to be a photographer and writer and artist in the land of California and San Francisco. For summer school in 1969 I took a photography class at San Francisco State and then ended up at City College of San Francisco instead of the Art Institute which in a sense was a much better choice for the type of social and political consciousness I was wanting.

In the summer where I took the photography class, I was excited to be on the campus where the student protest movement had been the spring before. There we developed and printed our work. We had an assignment, and I took streetcars and things over to the Golden Gate Bridge and snapped some photos of that. I didn't have a car, so it was hard for me to do that. I brought my marginal photographs back and developed them and printed them out and proudly featured them in class in front of a bunch of sophisticated and designer college talent that was far superior to my shallow perceptions of the world and I was nearly laughed out of class that day as they asked me "is that your idea of San Francisco—the Golden Gate Bridge?" Huge tears welled up in me as I rode the streetcar back to my apartment. I was totally humbled and then humiliated by my peers.

I'd been filled with hope and spirit and the desire to be important and talented. It was my way of trying to overcome having had a child out of wedlock and barely finishing high school, having an attempt on my life, and being rejected by important peers from high school.

In my second year of college at CCSF I was in a creative writing class. And after listening to a lot of academic rhetoric on how to write a story I decided to go home and spend the summer writing a short story and try to get it published. I wrote a piece entitled "Red, White and Blue Walls." I submitted it to **Aphra Women's Literary Magazine** and it was accepted and I was published in 1971. There it sat in Ferlenghetti's City Lights Bookstore in North Beach. I thought "Well maybe I can be a writer and have some depth." I became inflated from getting published and that sort of curtailed writing for a while except for journaling.

I couldn't afford a good camera and settled for checking them out of the film department at CCSF. They were 8x10 cameras with 8x10 negatives. Then there were two and a quarter cameras and negatives. I managed to do one fantastic art print of a friend's back using studio lights I checked out and quite by luck I created a stunning photograph and a professor at school bought it for $10.

There was something about my camera that allowed me to take risks and see new things. It gave me grace, courage, dignity, self-respect, and hope. It gave me a greater vision and I didn't have to be a fine artist.

These things were healing in terms of my isolation from the real world. The things I could have taken pictures of might have given me a sense of purpose an importance. It connected me to something: creativity, soul, purpose and the self-image of a photog or artist.

They would not have laughed me out of class for the photograph
I did of the Golden Gate Bridge and worked with in post-production.

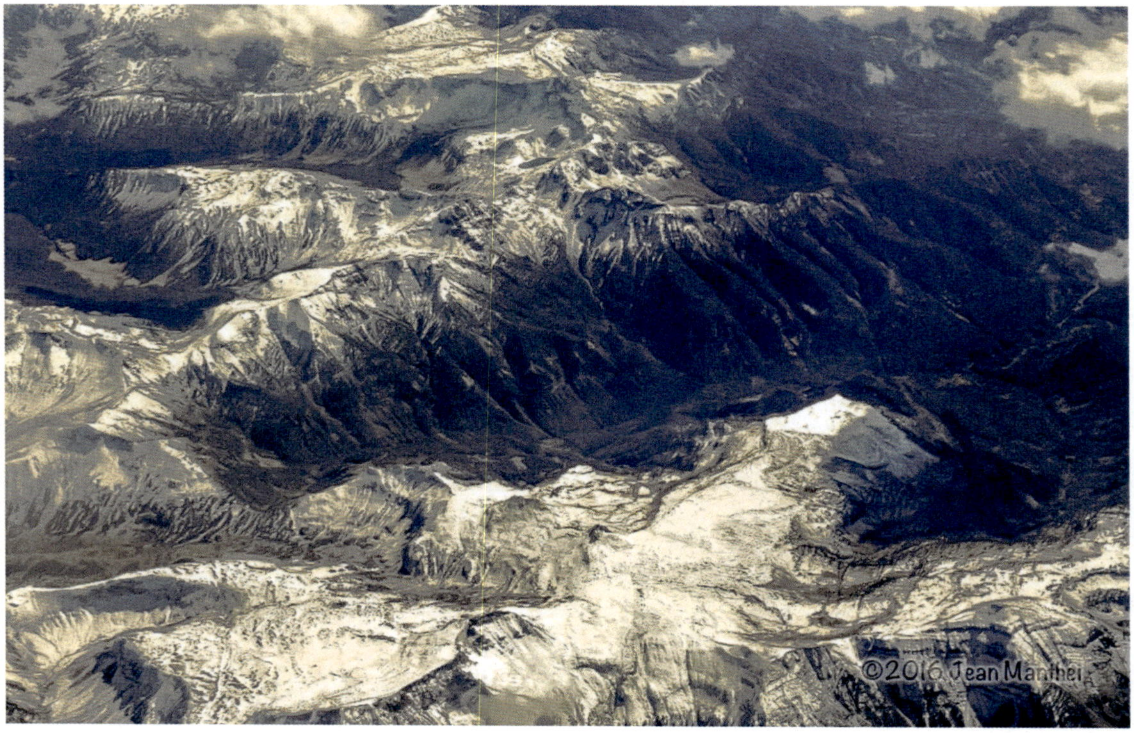
©2016 Jean Manthei

Then it was time to get serious in college. I decided I would never be as technically perfect as my peers who were photographing designer food and landscapes and commercial photographs. So, I relegated photography to the back burner for a while when I transferred to Lone Mountain College where I then changed my major to psychology and communications deciding instead to become a counselor where it would be more likely that I could support myself. I was also in intensive psychotherapy with some designer psychologist while I was in college which made a great impression on me.

Then after I graduated Magna Cum Laude in Psychology and Communications I dated a psychiatrist who was a police psychiatrist and he said, "we could have gone on you know." And I guess they must have because after I graduated there was a network of people who took me off the deep end and made me suicidal where I had to leave San Francisco and come home to my parents who seemed like they were the only people in the word who cared about me. I must have been an easy target and quite vulnerable. All the work I had done in therapy since the age of 13 seemed to be undone. When I went back to Colorado Springs, I ended up taking some secretarial classes as an alternative to totally decompensating and ending up at the state hospital. A clerical worker at the local mental health center told me to die after my suicide attempt.

I wasn't having very good experiences. I thought, as most college graduates, that I'd become a professional and be making a ton of money and be married and living happily ever after. Instead, I was watching the Mary Tyler Moore, Bob Newhardt and Mash shock treatments on Saturday night as I tried to overcome a sort of vegetative state. I did a whole lot of thought broadcasting and projecting and then discarded looking at the media. I think I stopped going to movies and watching much of anything on t.v. after seeing **Last Tango in Paris** right before I graduated from college. When I saw that film, I was speechless.

My photography was discarded. I was in a lot more treatment. All my dreams for the future were destroyed.

I ended up trying to get secretarial jobs and got fired and laid off from most of them. The people who had tried to kill me and made me suicidal seemed to be on the sidelines somewhere still affecting outcomes in my life.

I was too depressed to write or snap pictures. With another suicide attempt in 1979 I found myself with a diagnosis of Schizophrenia and Major Clinical Depression at the age of 29. I was hearing voices.

There were journals, but I didn't see a camera until 1985 when I earned enough money at a secretarial job to purchase a Pentax k1000. That was my first real camera—

a 35mm. I didn't get another one until 2000 and that was a Minolta 35mm. I really didn't have purpose or drive until I enrolled in the Counseling and Human Services program at University of Colorado Springs at Colorado Springs in 1988. I'd had a couple more decades of treatment and was on Social Security Disability. And I actually went through graduate school on the P.A.S.S. program (Program for Assisted Self-Support). Social Security helped me pay for graduate school along with government grants. It took me 4 years to get my Master's degree in Counseling and Human Services and I passed my LPC exam before graduating. But it took me another 5 years before I was able to get all my hours for my LPC and CACIII (now called CAS—Certified Addictions Specialist). I had to jump through all sorts of hoops for Department of Regulatory Agencies to prove I could practice with reasonable care and skill despite my disability. Public peril outweighs personal inconvenience. I had to get monitored supervision after a hospitalization in 1995 for a depressive episode from relapsing to smoking cigarettes. I've been practicing since 1993 and to tell you the truth I've never been able to make enough to support myself as an LPC, CAS. I've never been able to earn more than $800 to $1500 a month take home for my entire career. I've had to rely on other means to support myself. On what I earned full-time I could never have afforded car insurance, mortgage, medical bills and health insurance. We didn't get health benefits or sick leave or vacation pay.

The home I live in was provided for by my parents so I would not be homeless back in 1983.

There were a few pictures here and there after 1985. I didn't get a computer until I was 54 in 2004. I quit smoking cigarettes in 2002. When I did get my computer I soon after got a digital camera and I learned that photo companies would be places I could upload my photos and I found VioVio.com and started making photo books. I now had a recovery story to tell and eventually one of my photo books got published. That was **On Gratitude** which was part 8 in the series. I published that in 2010. I had a release party and invited everyone from work. My former minister came and said some prayers for my book. I then went to Nicotine Anonymous World Services Conference in 2013 and was elected to the Board as secretary. I flew all kinds of places between 2013 and 2016 and there was lots of things and places to take pictures of: out plane windows, beaches, cafes, landscapes, oceans. I would bring my camera, and this became a medium for expressing recovery ideas. I tell you my story because this impacts the topic of photography and schizophrenia. Knowing a little about me you might be able to get a sense of what motivates me behind the camera lens.

My photography during the years of 2002 to present really took form and purpose. I became a responsible schizophrenic and counselor with my camera and my work in the field as a counselor. I created an environment in my home of hospitality—pictures on the wall and my recovery dog of the century, Ketu.

I also made a photo book for clinicians in recent years in which I have a recovery idea or insight and picture. I show that to clients as a springboard for discussion or inspiration. I might show a picture of strawberries saying "You can't get strawberries in a hardware store" (you can't get honesty and integrity at a bar or concert). They are pictures and idioms expressing recovery ideas for clients suffering from AOD disorders. I called it ***Recovery Book for Clinicians.***

I did a grief journey to Carmel, CA in 2016 to heal and do some grief work for the loss of my family over a period of 15 years. I ended up with some stupendous pictures of rough, crashing seas and landscapes and two rocks in particular, that looked like they were in an embrace. My photography then spoke of grief issues.

My photographs told stories about healing from grief, tragedy, deep therapeutic thought in pictures, expressions of humor and love when I couldn't get love. There was also authenticity that was emerging. I discovered the here and now when I wasn't smoking and that was present in my photography. Then I learned of some photogs that were working with the concepts of Zen and Tao and contemplative photography. I found photogs that were willing to explore spirituality in photography—prayer in photography. And I discovered my own work was starting to have presence and depth. This indeed was part of the healing forces at work in assuming responsibility and staying in remission.

Several years ago, I'd enter contests to try and win a camera and none of my pictures were ever deemed prize worthy by the prize experts. I instead had to earn the money to buy a Rebel T3i camera and then eventually a 70D and now a 6D Mark II. Between 2002 and 2008 I got into camcorders and documenting my own day-to-day struggles with overcoming tobacco addiction which I attribute to some of my success in staying off cigarettes and remission from my illness.

The photographs you see here in my work came about from being in the moment and thinking outside the box. I was able to try a lot of presets in Lightroom, Polarr, Luminar, Pixelmator, Affinity, Topaz Impressions, Effects and Textures. OnOne was pretty good as well as Comic Life. Post-production was able to do what my camera couldn't. And they made ordinary shots extraordinary.

Maybe because I have schizophrenia, they are more interesting to my reader—in mainstream society, would they compete substantially? I became a member of Scott Kelby's Photoshop Kelby One. But I couldn't win any of their contests either.

You'll see here some respectable photographs of the Golden Gate Bridge that I got when I was in San Francisco at the NicA World Services Conference in 2015. And they wouldn't get laughed out of a photography class now. Designer schizophrenic photos?

I think they're more just expressions of my illness, pain, joy, PTSD, grief and ways of overcoming difficulty and hardships lifting myself up to something higher. I'm always looking for meaning in things—the Golden Gate Bridge was a rite of passage bridge. For clients, when I show them a picture of the Golden Gate bridge—I tell them "Eventually you have to get off the bridge and walk the talk of recovery—it's a whole new land and another language."

There was something about starting a book like this and writing the first 12-13 pages. I was left feeling agitated, hopeless, and depressed as memories flooded me while I was up and down with the CPAP machine. My usual, easy going self was now agitated and filled with the red flags of decompensation. Had I been thinking I might have picked up my camera and shot some pictures. But I wasn't motivated to do that. Earlier this week with red flags of decompensation I went to Mesa Lookout Point and waited for some cloud wisps to appear around the mountains, but they didn't. And there were some people there smoking and seeming to harass me, so I left. I got some marginal mountain photos that a tourist would have delighted in, but which did not move me, and I left. It is possible that in these types of moments that picking up my camera is when it would be most healing. Tomorrow I'm getting a moon filter to use on the telescope with the camera attached to get more effective images of the moon phases and the moon with craters.

In January I got Blood Moon pictures that reminded me of an umbilical cord. The photo book I was working on for clients and clinicians to use before a group was given birth to and released as to any expectations for success. Now it is just securing permissions to use photographs I snapped of the Golden Gate Bridge or the Long Beach skyline and the Native American rattle and a French Horn to use in my book. Was waiting for a literary agent to get back to me about getting it published. And I will have to buy commercial licenses for any Adobe Stock images I bought with my membership and planted myself in flying my drone if I was to get published [but I didn't buy any Adobe Stock images to use—I used all of my own work except childhood and school photos].

© 2019 Jean Manthei

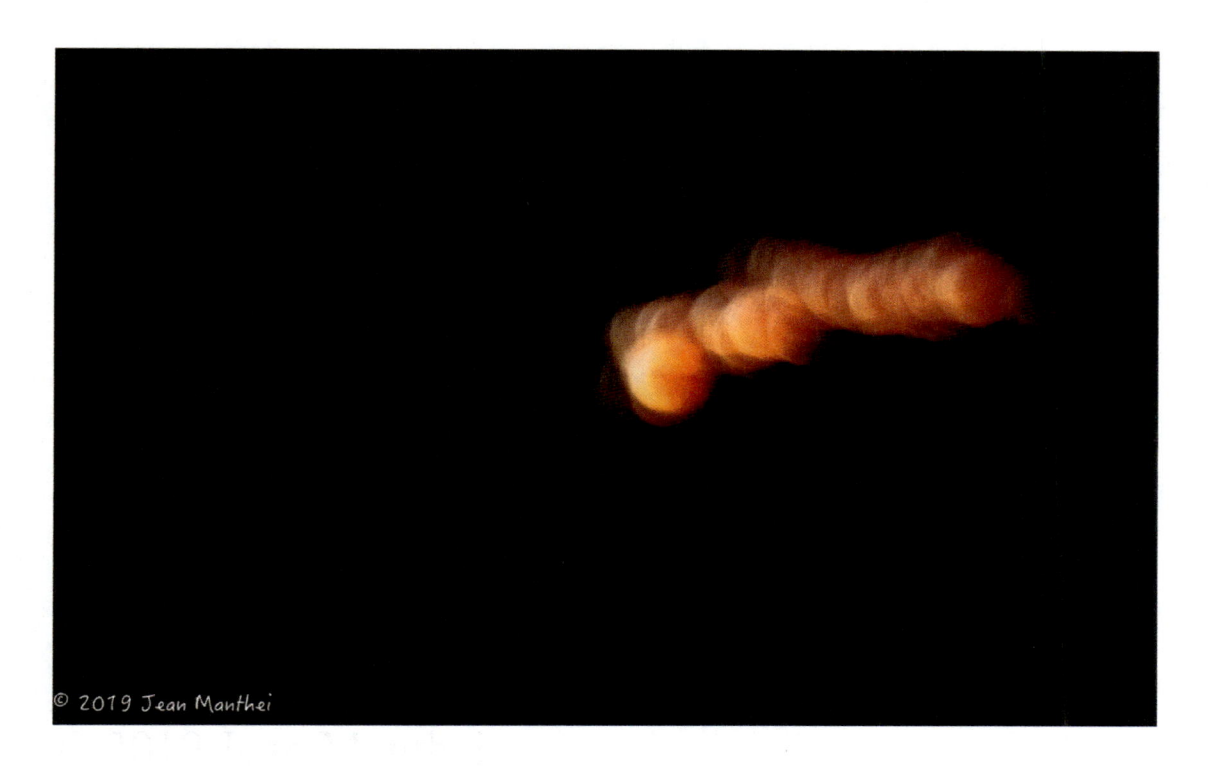

The Blood Moon in January 2019 that to Jean seemed like an umbilical cord and the one that she let go of and which gave birth to **Recovery Book for Clinicians** and **Photography and Schizophrenia.**

So, photography and schizophrenia: as one becomes healthier with this illness photographs begin to represent more integration and wholeness. The photographs get well with you.

I haven't been in the hospital since 1995 and that had been my first serious attempt at quitting tobacco. I had relapsed after 6 weeks "smober." I became very depressed and had to go to the hospital. I hadn't been snapping many pictures back then. I think I'd take pictures when I went to visit my parents in California at Christmas time. We'd go to Laguna Beach. I was thrilled to snap pictures of the sea even though it was a tourist trap. In 1985 they took me to El Capistrano Mission near San Diego. I got pictures of a beautiful stone fountain and then that fountain with pigeons around it.

Just because of the one hospitalization for relapse to cigarettes that made me depressed I had to jump through all sorts of hoops for Department of Regulatory Agencies to prove I could practice with reasonable skill and care.

I also have some photographs I will group here that I snapped as well as friends took back in high school at Judson School in Arizona and La Chatelainie in St. Blaise, Switzerland [the La Chatelainie pictures are now missing (but I did find them and will scan a few in here]. In some ways my photographs were incongruent with the pain I had inside of me and the trauma and illness that might have been brewing.

I got this dog from the Humane Society in 2000 after my other dog Solo passed away. Ketu (key to my heart which is what I called her) and I had a rough couple of years where she chewed up a comforter and pillows and other objects until I took her to Bark Busters where we got the "who is boss" worked out. Then I fell in love with Ketu and she was the recovery dog of the century.

26

Used by permission of Capistrano Mission near San Diego.
Picture by Jean Manthei, Circa 1987.

Her ghost spirit is still in this house watching over Honey and I. She saw me in the last two years I smoked cigarettes. And then I quit in 2002 and Ketu was my absolute best friend and confidant. I snapped quite a few beautiful pictures of Ketu and that was my way of establishing a meaningful relationship with my dog. One Christmas in 2011, after my book had been published, I did a photo of Ketu looking at her picture in ***On Gratitude*** where I say in the book that such creatures never use domestic violence or verbal assault on you. And later I wrote "Ketu is good with schizophrenic authors" and scrawled that over the photograph and put it on a 16x20 print that hangs in my living room to this day.

I also made a comic strip in one of the comic apps and put that on a pillow. It says "Photoshop cures schizophrenia, alcoholism and smoking. Photoshop instead of psychosis."

"I'm schizophrenic, but I'm highly educated and I'm well-trained and I don't talk in word salads, I make sense, I'm responsible and I'm not psychotic--look--see here I am looking responsible, stable and creative.

My photography took off with the love of Ketu and now with Honey.

My photography was integrating some complex ideas and recovery knowledge.

Right now, I'm waiting for purple Calla Lilies' to come which I will take pictures of. I've been waiting a day for them. They were to cheer me up and say congrats for the ***Recovery Book for Clinicians*** that I made the 2nd edition of and this one ***Photography and Schizophrenia*** that I began work on yesterday. Calla Lilies' came a day late and I'm due to get another bunch tomorrow because they were late. I snapped some fantastic pictures of them after yelling at my camera because it wasn't working right and then the flash didn't work and then it did. I hurt the feelings of the Calla Lilies' and they might have been more disturbed by the harsh way I talked to the camera than the freezing weather. Now they are being calmed by Baroque and Beyond.

I was in ***Pieces of Mind*** a few years ago which was an exhibition that featured the work of people with mental illness---paintings, photography, sculpture. They put on this exhibit each year between 2004 and 2008. I sold a print for $250 of a forest scene out at Benet Pines in the Black Forest where I went on a retreat to celebrate a year of recovery from cigarettes back in 2003. In 2008 I snapped a photo out of the plane on the way back from California coming into Colorado of some great mountain ranges. That was on the last visit I had with my mom before she passed away the following May 2008. The **Pieces of Mind** exhibit awarded it to a state legislator.

Because I have schizophrenia and have suffered some of the things I have I'd expect my art and photography to be filled with something like shards of glass or lots of broken things because I had been broken and broken into. I don't think my work is the dark and depressing work that a person would ordinarily expect from someone with schizophrenia. I think my work is more uplifting than it is depressing. But I've also had 60 years of treatment and am a responsible schizophrenic, counselor and I exercise that responsibility when I photograph things. When I passed the 50th anniversary of having been in treatment I threw a party to celebrate a half a century of treatment. My minister, some friends and several of the counselors who have worked me while I have lived in Colorado were there.

I was trying to think if you could interpret photography as an analyst would interpret dreams. Are there images that portend illness, death and the onset of psychosis, over-inflation or grandiosity in my work? Really, I think the things I do are representing stability and responsibility and giving me sanity and self-respect. There are a few photographs that could represent illness, death or depression. I've continued in therapy. I became a counselor in my own right—an LPC and CAS (before known as CACIII). I stay on my meds. I work at self-care and responsible thinking so there shouldn't be fragmented and incoherent pieces anymore in my collections. I don't think I have any actively psychotic work. An exception. Once when I was 16, I painted a picture that won first prize and I got a paint set. The picture had unexplained and unintended images of people hidden in the black and blue splotches with broken mirrors sprinkled on the painting. Certainly,

Here are some shards of glass for you if you need to see a schizophrenic with shards of broken glass. I bought this Photoshop template called Broken and placed my photo in it. It's quite effective. My photography is a little more hopeful than that. This could represent psychosis or decompensation.

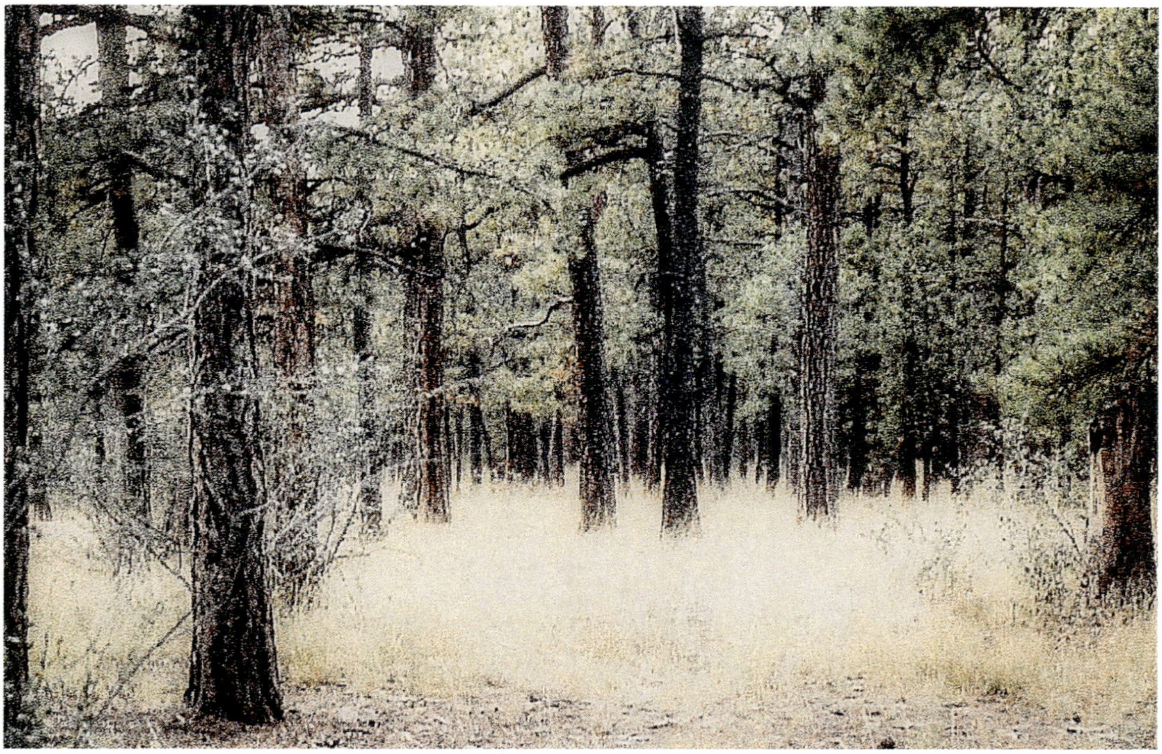

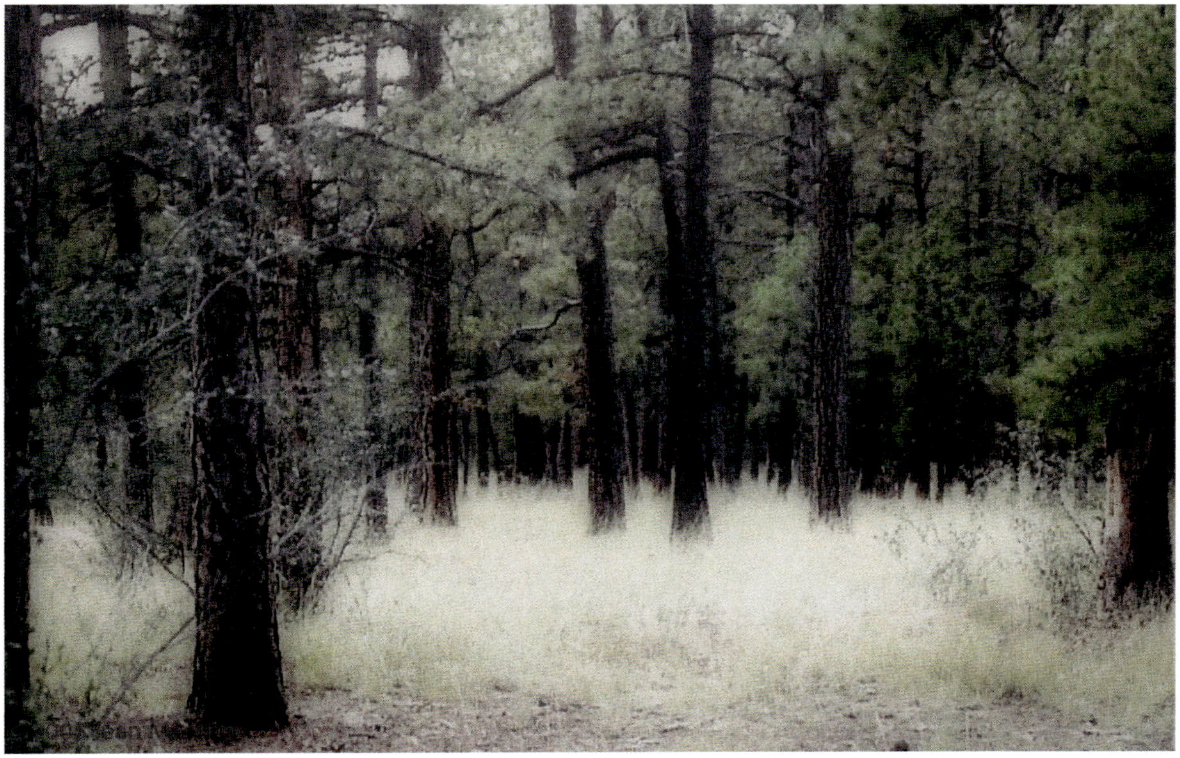

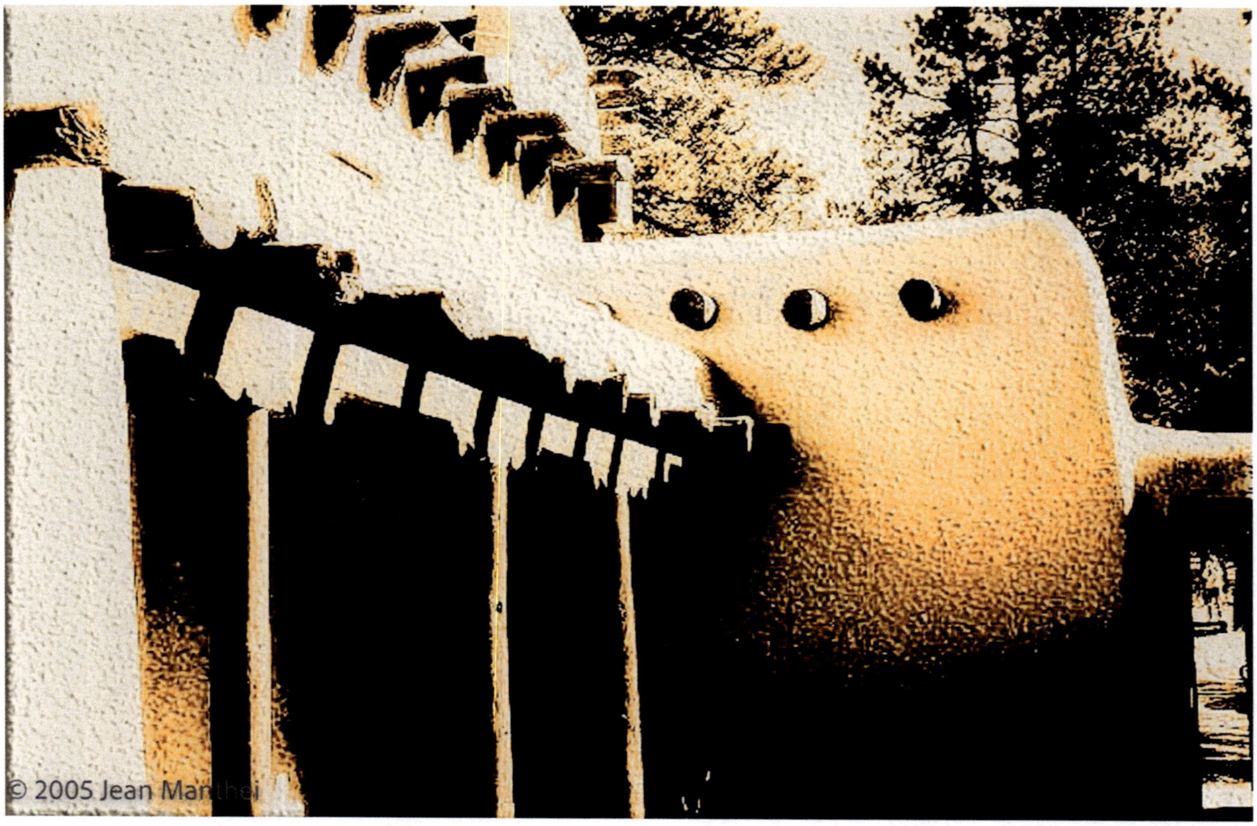
© 2005 Jean Manthei

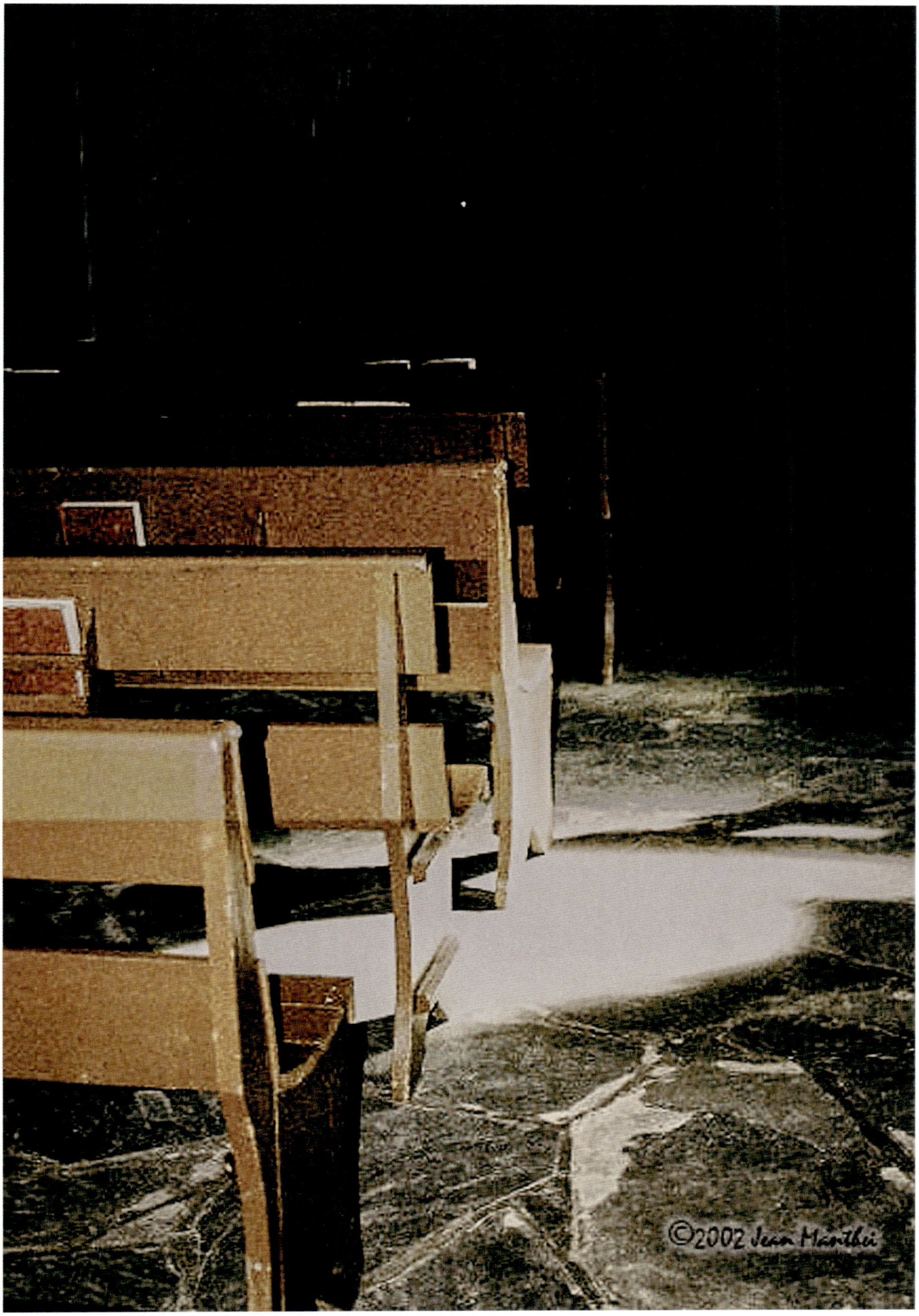
©2002 Jean Mänthei

© 2016 Jean Manthei

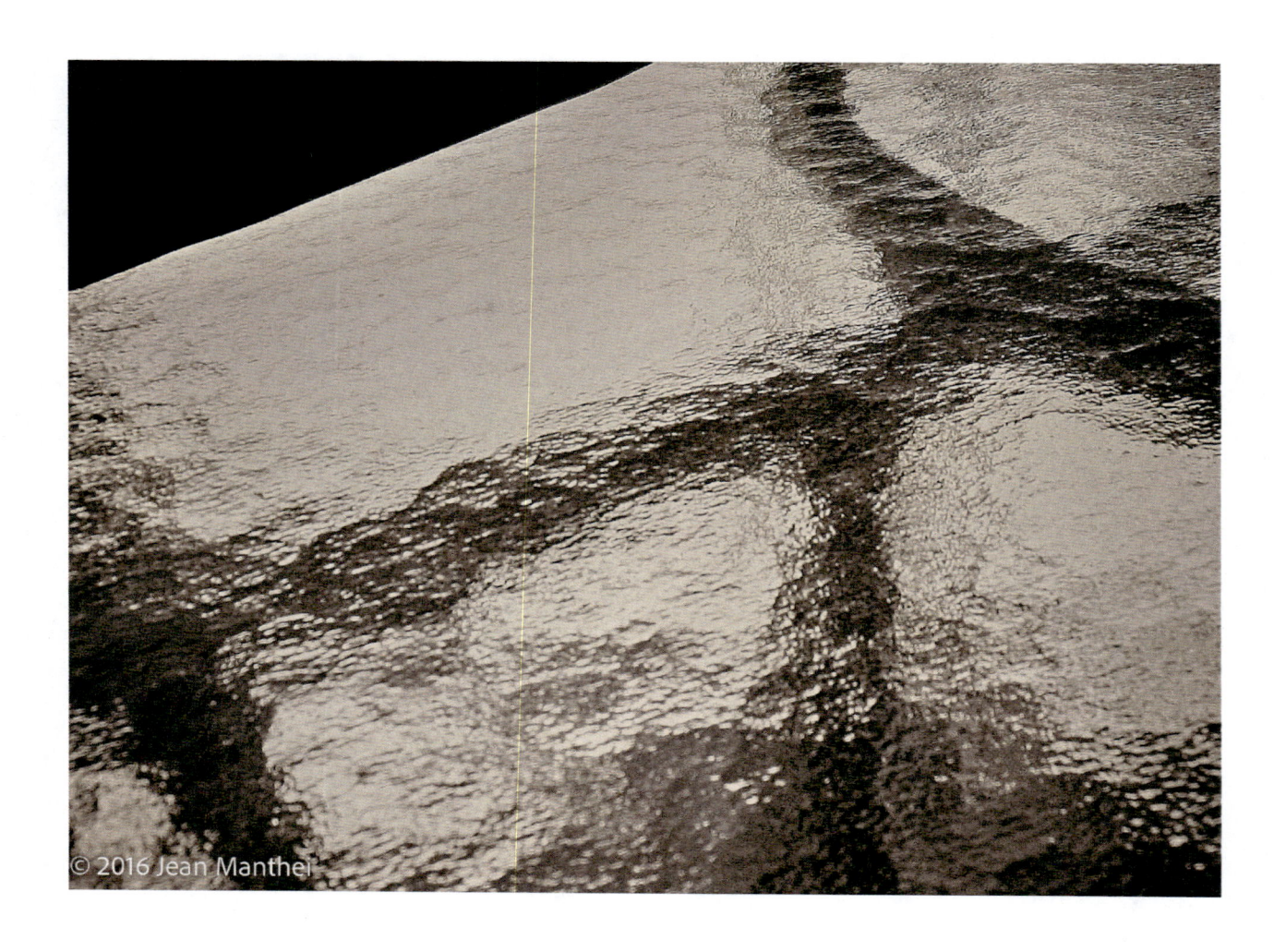

© 2021 Jean Manthei

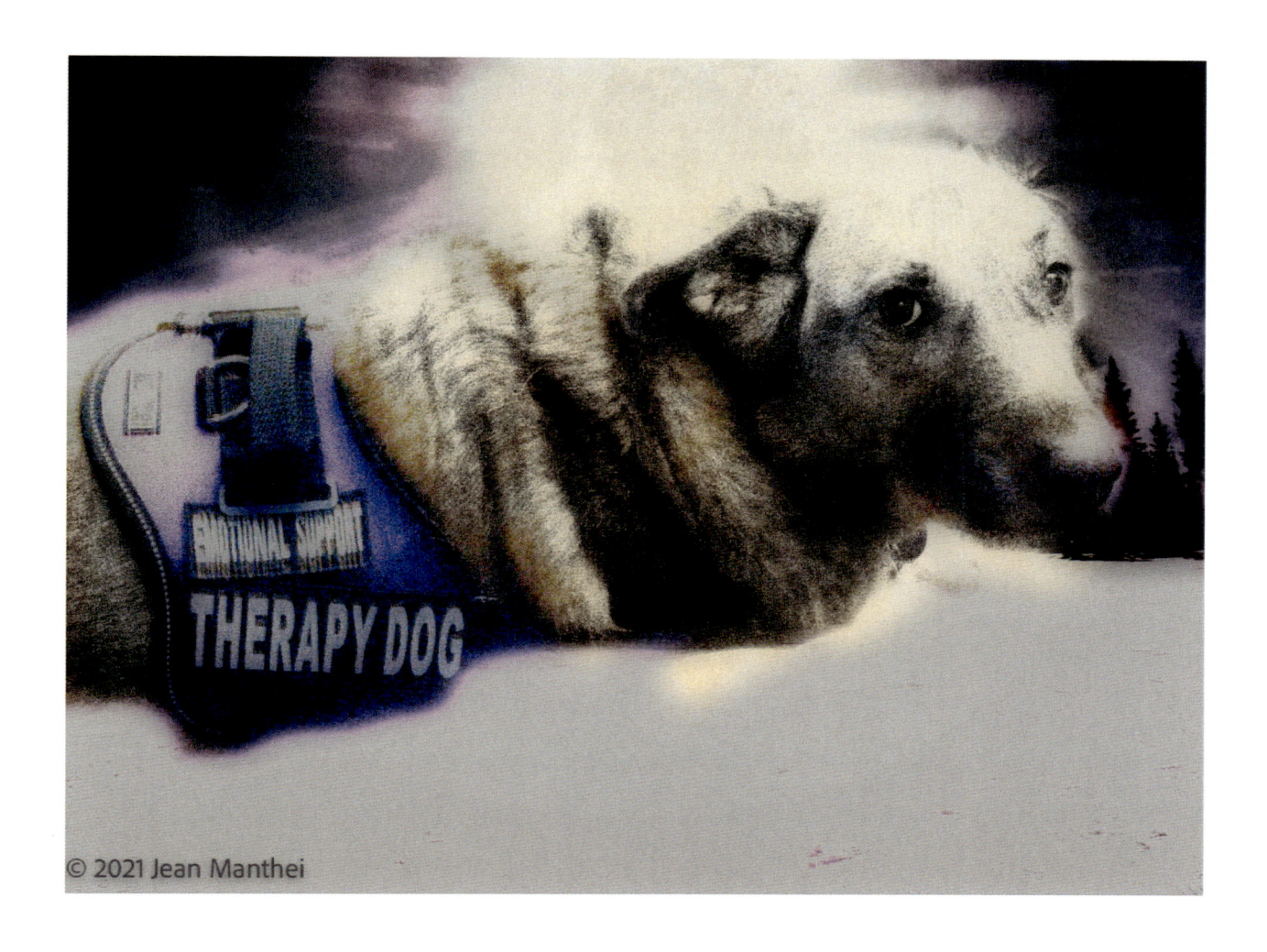

that painting had been a work of genius for a 16 year old, but could have predicted later tragedy and psychosis and hopelessness. It was right before I had had my child. Maybe when one is being responsible and whole there is lack of depth. According to Lawrence Kubie (circa 1965) who wrote ***The Neurotic Distortion of the Creative Process***, the person with neurosis is afraid to give up their neurosis because they fear they will give up their creativity (Kubie, 1965). Kubie (1965) said that a person has much more access to their resources and unconscious when not neurotic. The same type of thinking can be applied to psychosis and addiction—that the person suffering from psychosis, addiction or other illness is afraid to give up their psychosis or addiction because they will give up their creativity—when in fact one has much more access to their unconscious and the power of making responsible social or political and psychological statements with their art if not overcome by metaphor, Puff the Magic Dragon, psychosis and so on. People sometimes think they need their disability or their illness and psychiatric symptoms or intoxication and deficits to create real art or the art would be shallow and superficial. I think the opposite is true, as Kubie would assert (Kubie, 1965).

At a loss for interpreting my own work on some levels. When I take pictures or write—it's not to say "how can I achieve depth here?" It is that I am more likely to think "how can this be something that achieves meaning?"

In a mental health art exhibit people expect to see deep and disturbing images from mental patients. They hunger for things they can read incredible meaning in. People that exploit say that sort of thing sells and brings in the crowds.

Another thought I had was that while snapping pictures in Carmel, CA in 2016—100s of other people were snapping pictures of the same rough seas and rocks. If they featured their work somewhere—people would enjoy it. If I were to enter another mental health exhibition and feature

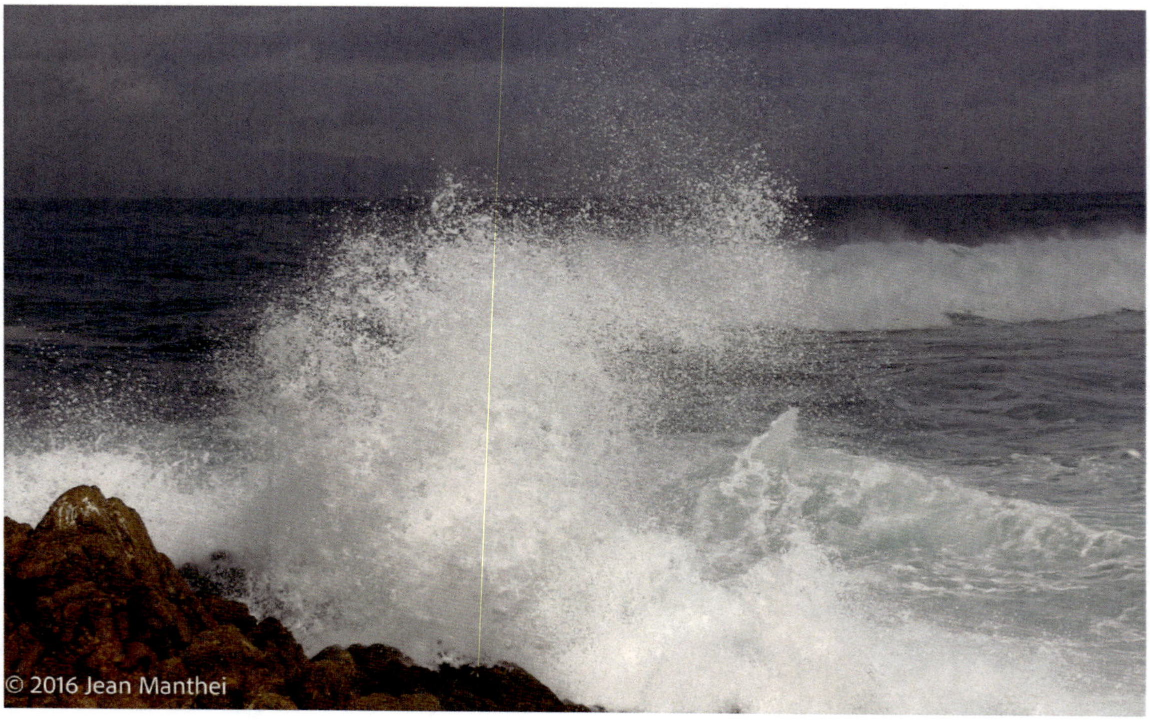
© 2016 Jean Manthei

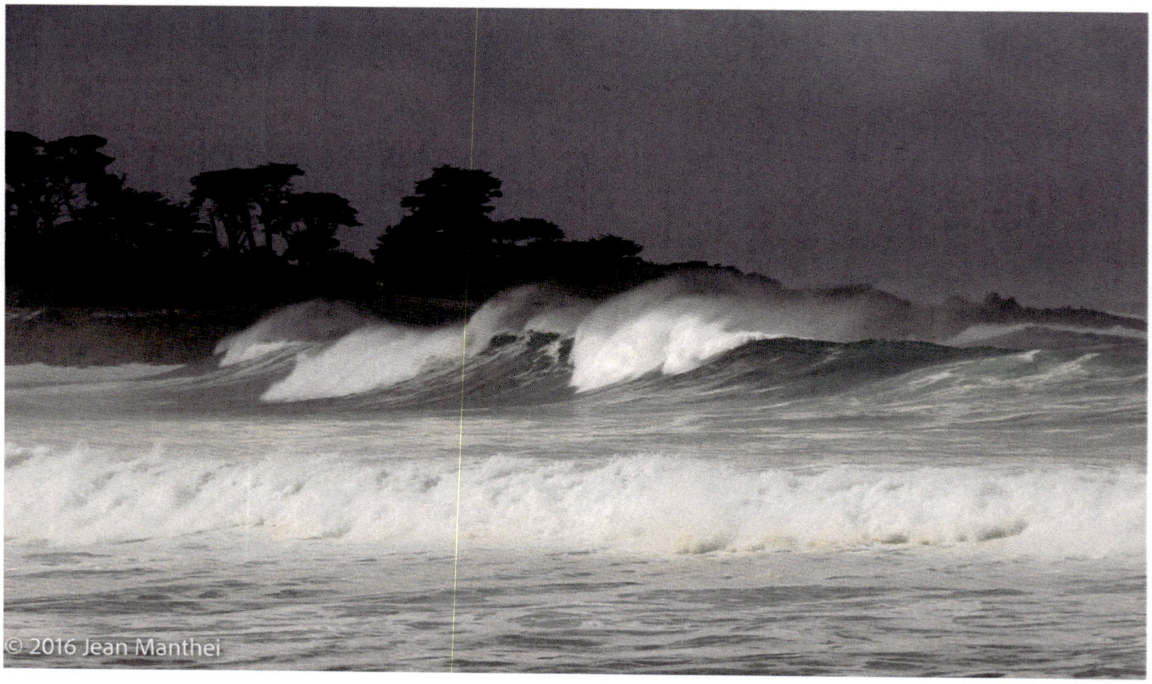
© 2016 Jean Manthei

© 2016 Jean Manthei

© 2016 Jean Manthei

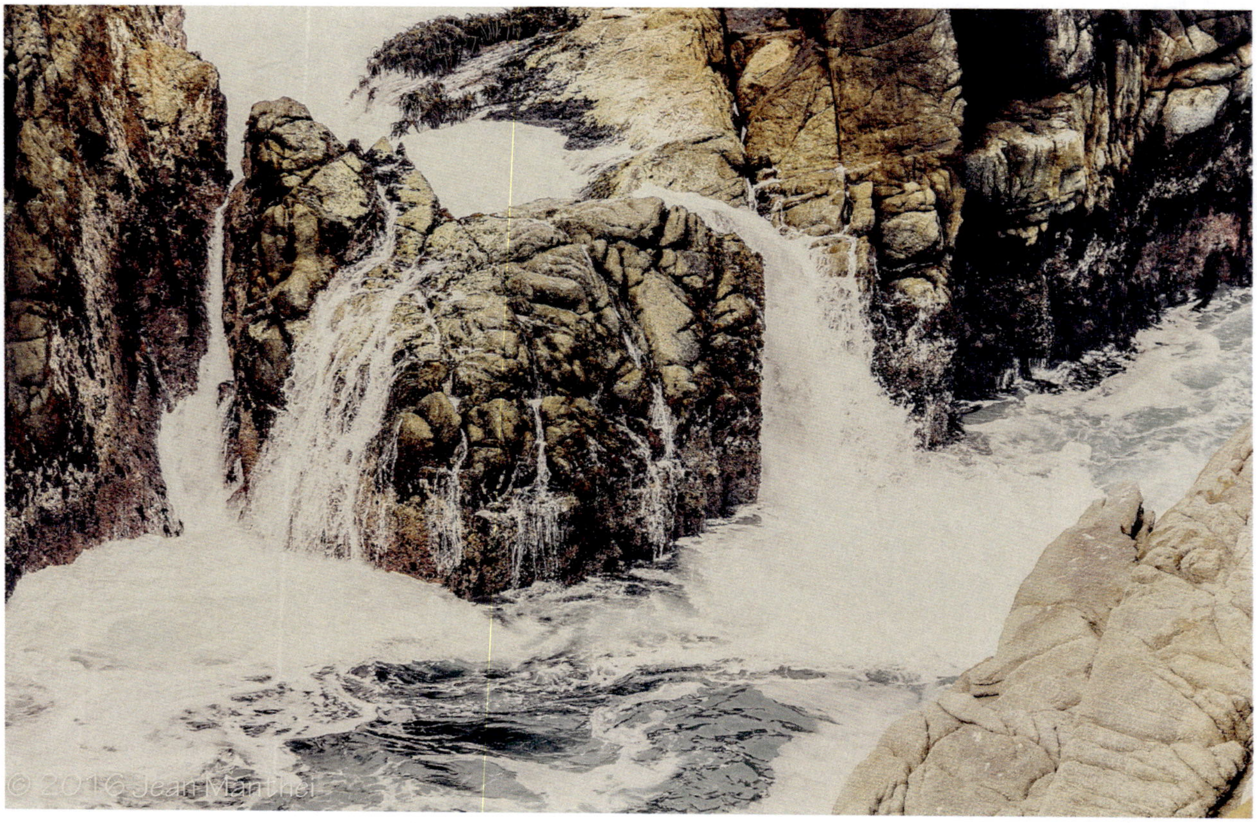
© 2016 Jean Manthei

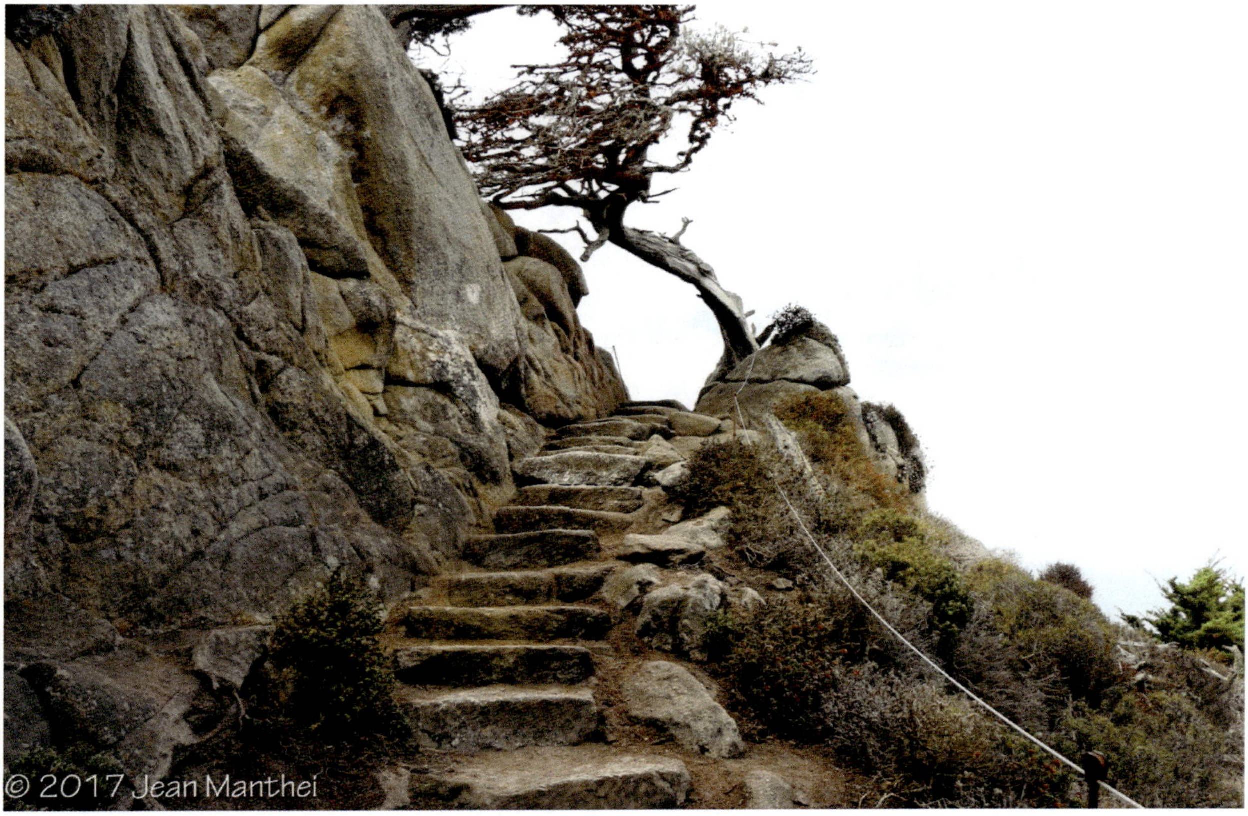
© 2017 Jean Manthei

The two rocks in an embrace. If you look you will see a pile of rocks--if you look again, you will see love.

© 2016 Jean Manthei

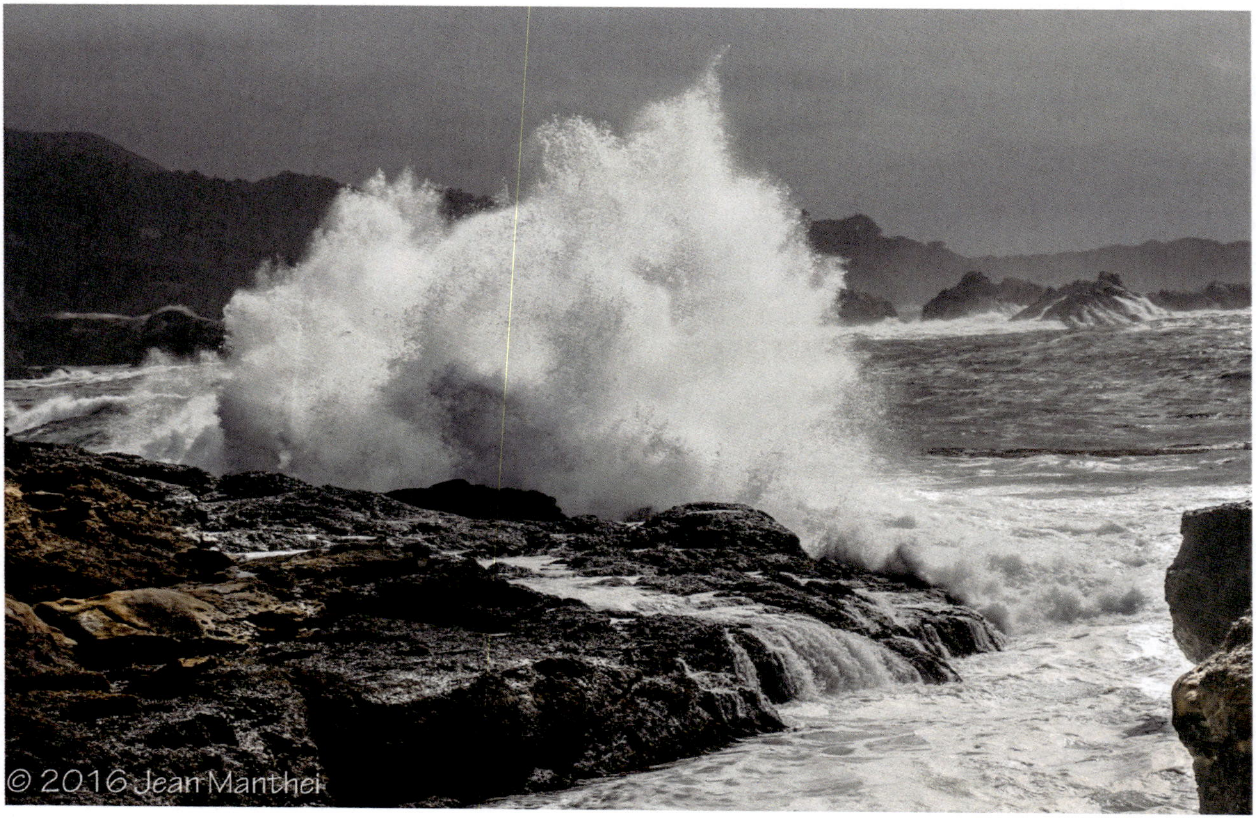
© 2016 Jean Manthei

my interpretation of the crashing seas in Carmel, would it suddenly become more novel because a schizophrenic snapped the picture? Why is that? Perhaps the fact that I have schizophrenia and work at photography and have some achievements under my belt and some experience that maybe the things I snap pictures of might be more compelling because it raises questions and maybe even answers questions about creativity and mental illness to overcome such difficulties and illness and do the things that other people do and take for granted. Are there hidden gems in my work that are not in the work of a talented normie? I don't know the answer to these questions. Then why have exhibits featuring the work and art of people with mental illness?

If I take pictures of crashing seas or a lone boat does that portend hardship or death and illness in the schizophrenic, but not in someone who is normal? If it doesn't portend psychosis and death in the normie then why should it in me just because I have schizophrenia?

If I have schizophrenia and portray responsible and healthy photographs what does that mean? Does this predict health and well-being? Stability? Even with the dread disease of schizophrenia? Does it predict a good prognosis? Could people with mental disorders use their photography as tools to strive toward integration and well-being instead of amplifying disturbing images, colors, and textures? Not all schizophrenia is disturbing and fragmented. I also think schizophrenia can create other beautiful realities and visions that are not psychotic and disturbed, but perhaps quite heathy and interesting, leading to new connections between thoughts and creating new ideas. Not all chaos is psychotic. In schizophrenia the danger is that you stay in the chaos.

It was Karl Menninger (circa 1950s) that asked what was right with clients and what are they doing to successfully cope rather than what are they doing that is pathological and destructive? Could photography and other art be used in the service of being predictors of client strengths in the face of adversity—predictors of health and well-being and things they are doing right? Could photography be a means of expressing what is right and the expression of strengths?

The Calla Lilies' didn't perish from my hysterical efforts to get good pictures. They have recovered substantially with **Baroque and Beyond** and Robert Aubrey Davis's interesting voice and style.

I have an exercise for you since all the photog books I have read of late have exercises for their readers. This is an unusual one.

I want you to imagine that you have schizophrenia, and your symptoms might be depression, voices or thinking errors. You might be frightened. You might be feeling hopeless. Perhaps your dreams have been stripped from you and you don't know what to do or who to go to, but you have a phone and it has a camera—maybe you have a camera—thanks be to God. What would take a picture of that would capture voices or thinking errors? If you took a picture of yourself—what would it say about you if you had the dread disease of schizophrenia? How would you think you would look? Would there be anything you would take a picture of that would help you to overcome such overwhelming odds and feelings?

If you were thinking "life is unfair, I've been cheated—I didn't get what I deserved"; what would you be likely to photograph? If you were thinking "what goes around comes around" what would you take a picture of? How would you convey that resentment? How might you overcome those fears and resentments and anger? How would your phone or camera bring you back to reality and allow you to feel bigger or more grounded and whole?

Now imagine you have Antisocial Personality Disorder and Substance Use Disorder Moderate or some other addiction and you're hungry, angry and lonely and tired and you are 5 days sober. What are you angry about and how would you use your camera to snap pictures of that anger in a creative way to work with your anger, urges and cravings?

What picture might captivate you? What if you were 90 days sober and just simply feeling gratitude? What would the picture then be?

Now imagine you have Borderline Personality Disorder and issues with identity and finding your path and who you are: how would you explore identity with your camera?

And then imagine you have Major Clinical Depression. How would you use a camera or a phone to capture that despair and then bring hope back into the picture? How would you snap a picture of a hopeful experience?

Imagine you have Obsessive-Compulsive Personality Disorder? What picture would help you work through obsessions and compulsions with either addictions, compulsions, self, relationships, work, or personality?

If there isn't much more to say on the topic of photography and schizophrenia, then there isn't. I thought there might be and why I picked up my pen again this afternoon.

I thought, dear reader, in the event, that I have no more to say on the topic that you would enjoy the photography of a bonafide schizophrenic counselor who has had a chemical imbalance since birth. Just looking at all this knowing that a schizophrenic made this up and snapped all these pictures and made this connection between schizophrenia and photography could make you happy and would give you something to think about and wonder around for weeks pondering. And you could tell your kids or friends about this wonder patient and say there is truly some hope if you lose it and go off the deep end because one can always buy a camera, a journal and a scrapbook to share your story with anyone who will listen and not be judgmental and hostile and aggressive.

©2016 Jean Manthei

2017 Jean Manthei

© 2005 Jean Manthei

© 2020 Jean Manthei

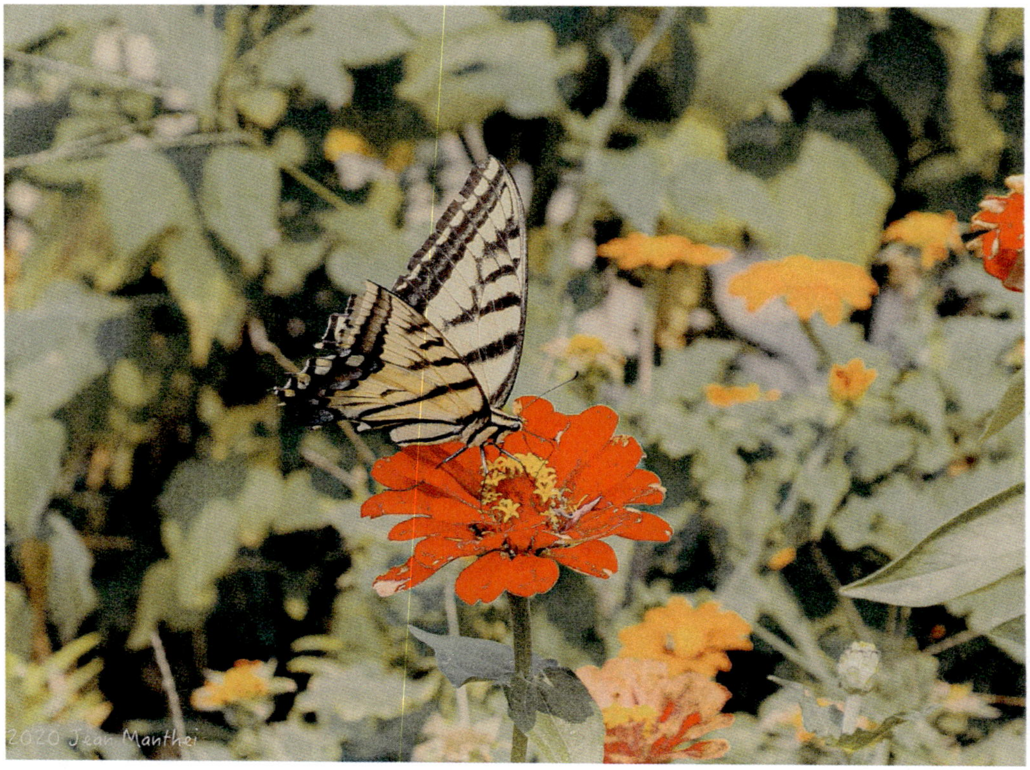
2020 Jean Manthei

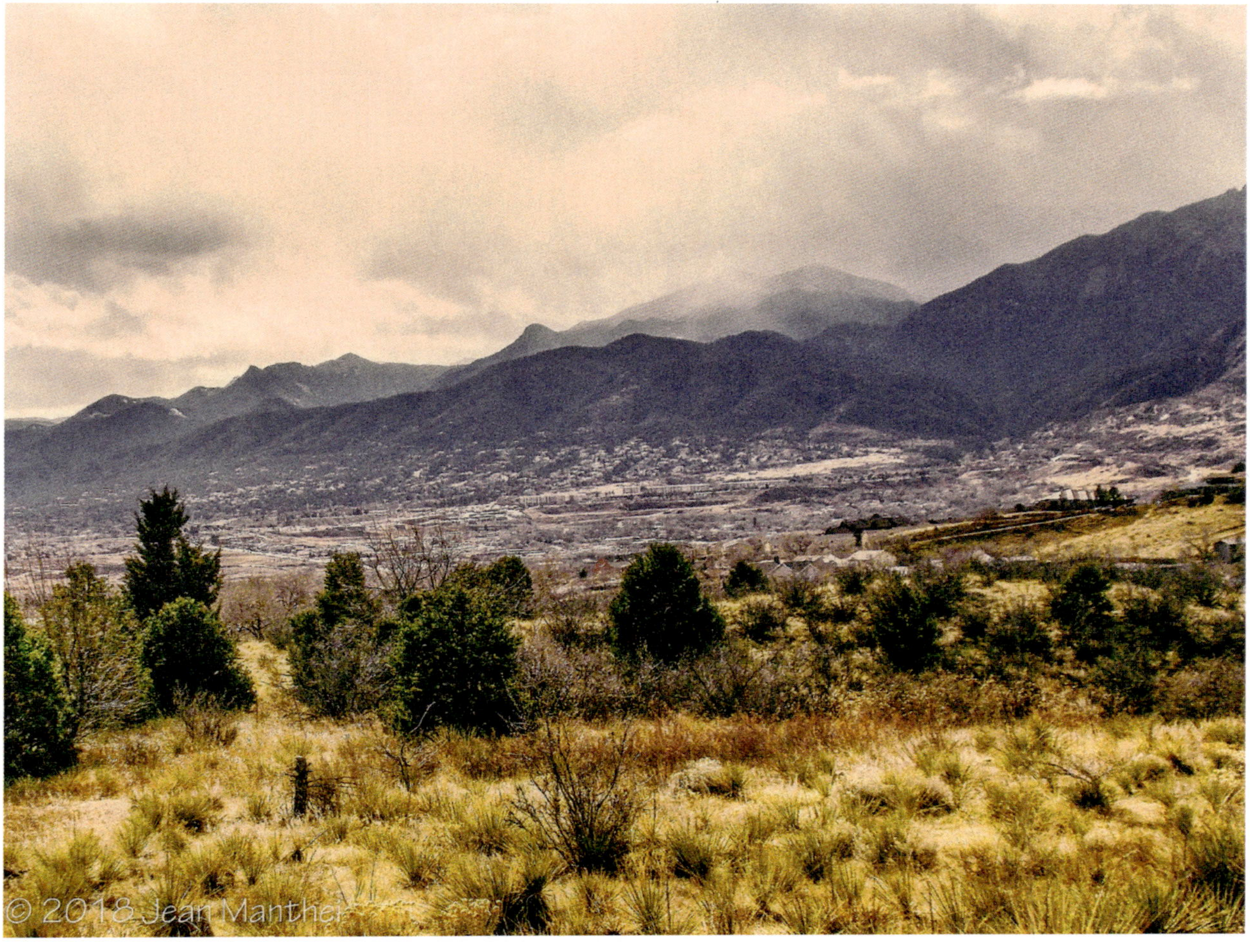
© 2018 Jean Manthei

I dropped a moon into my photograph of the Garden of the Gods. It's my moon. I dropped some clouds into it--they're my clouds. Things like that can be playful and fun and bring joy to your creativity. It's just simple things. My photograph is not as exceptional as the Adobe Stock image, but it's mine. So, my book was just to reflect the photographs of someone with schizophrenia--not creating something fantastic with Adobe Stock images. These reflect my skills good and marginal--but it's all okay.

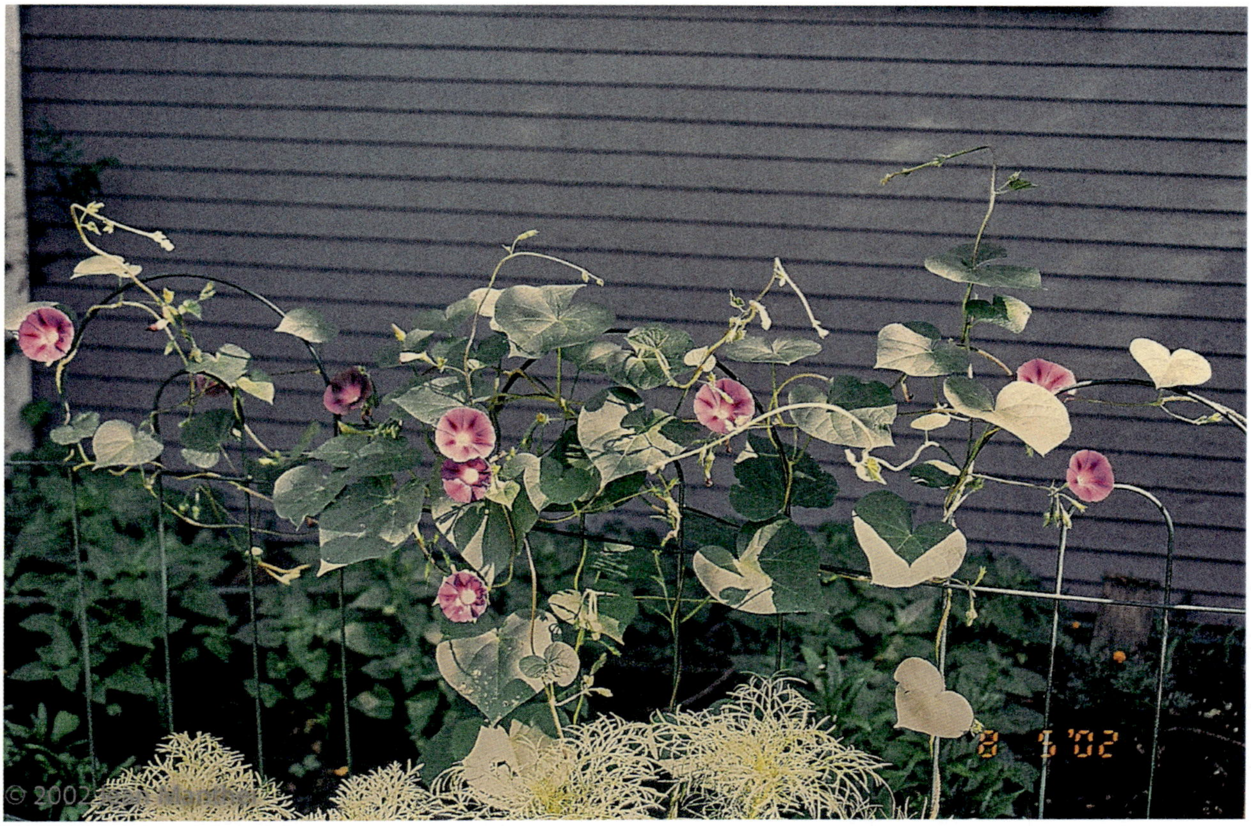
© 2002
8 5 '02

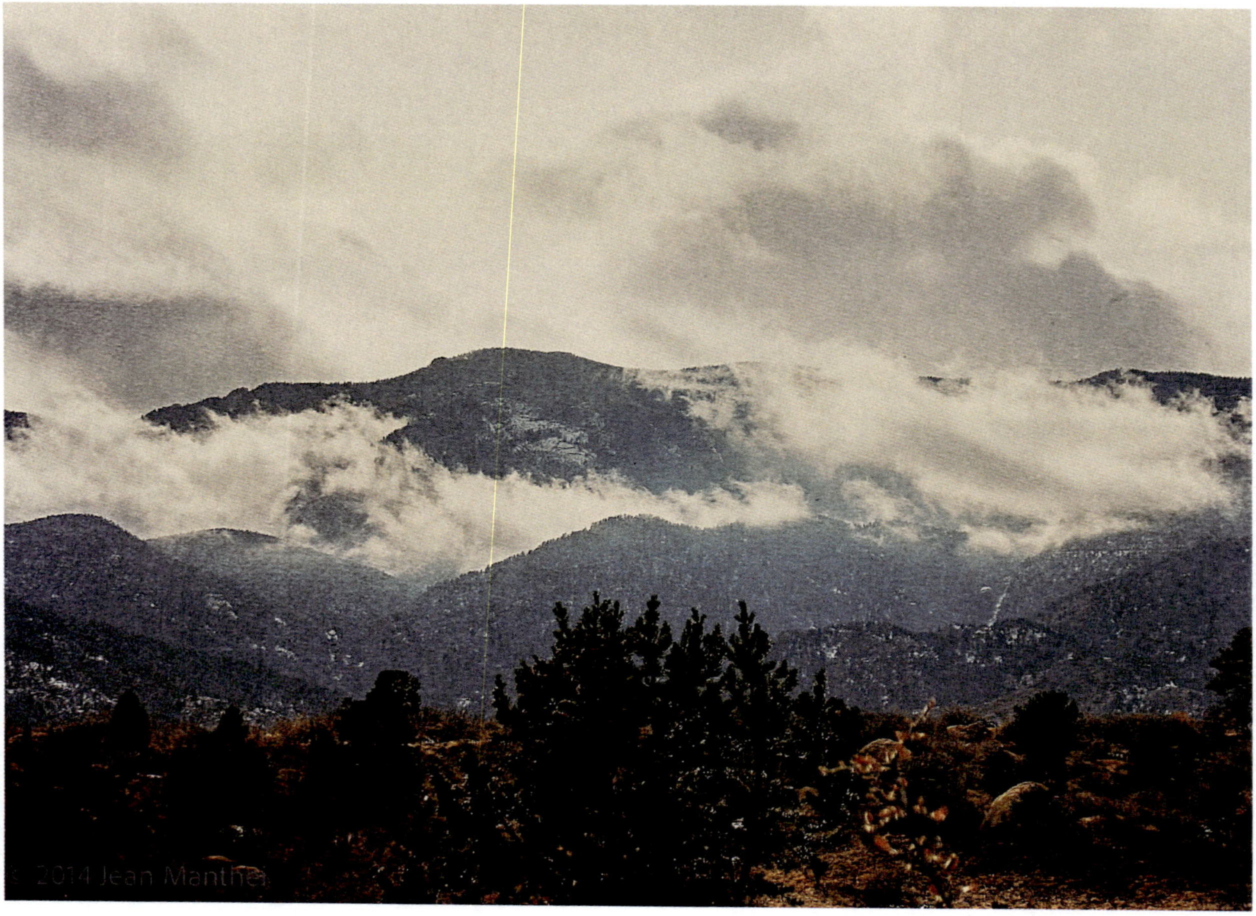
© 2014 Jean Manthei

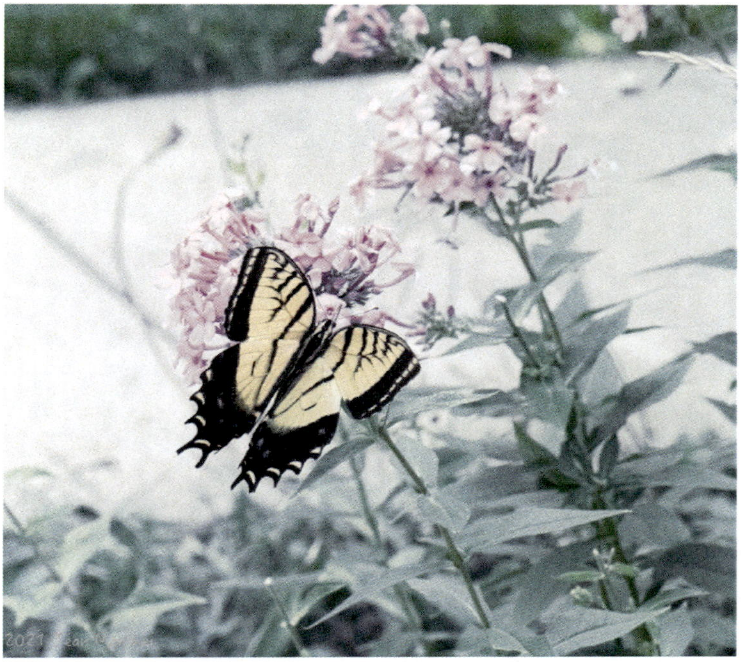

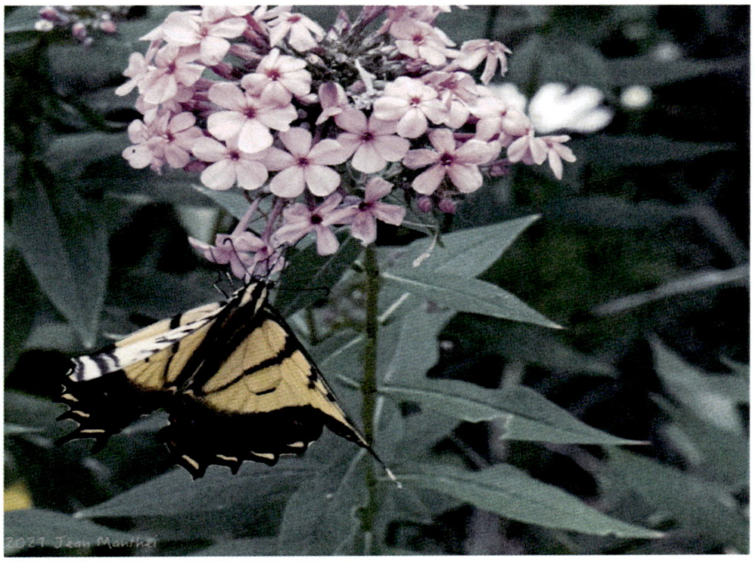
2021 Jean Manthei

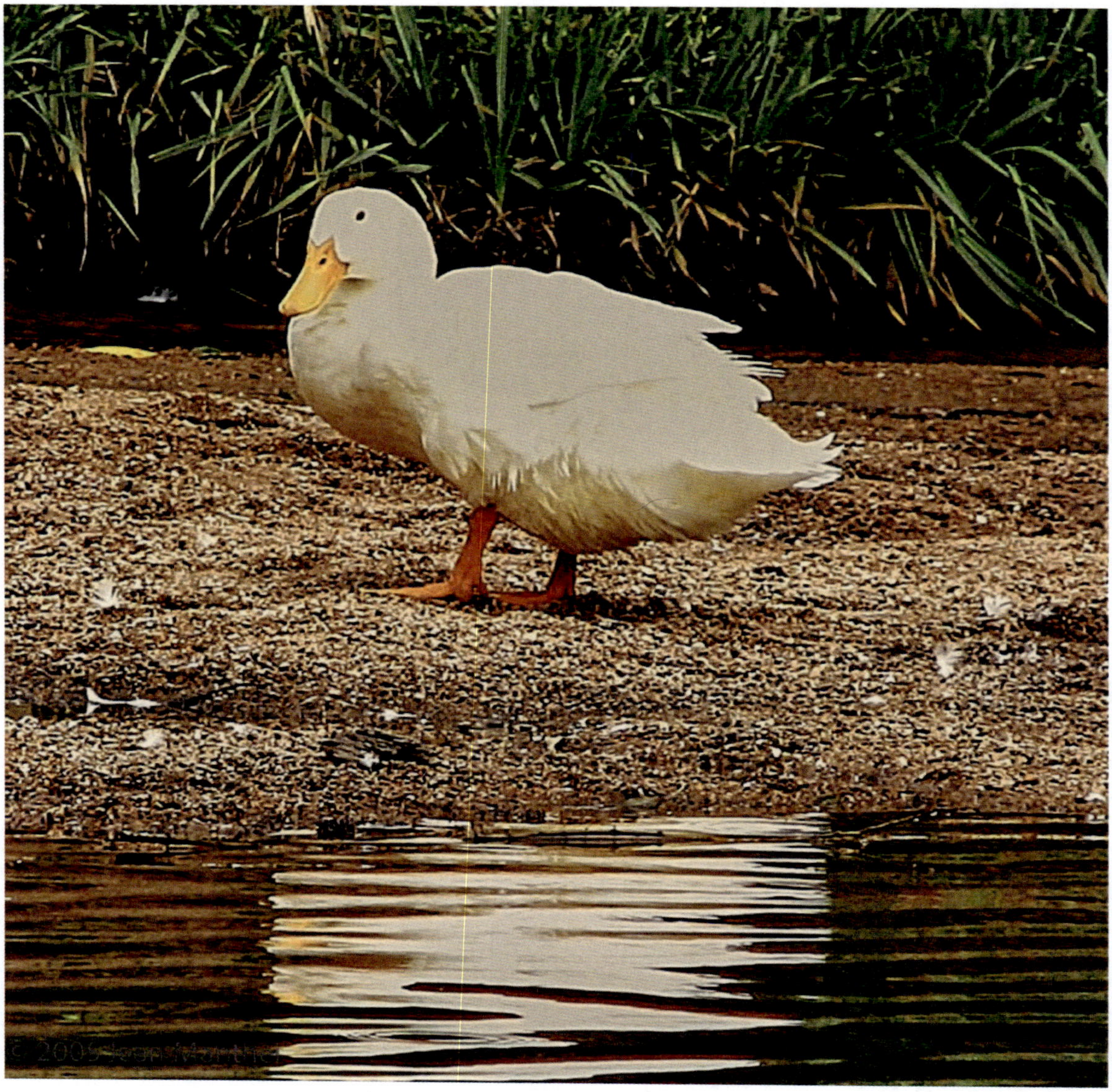

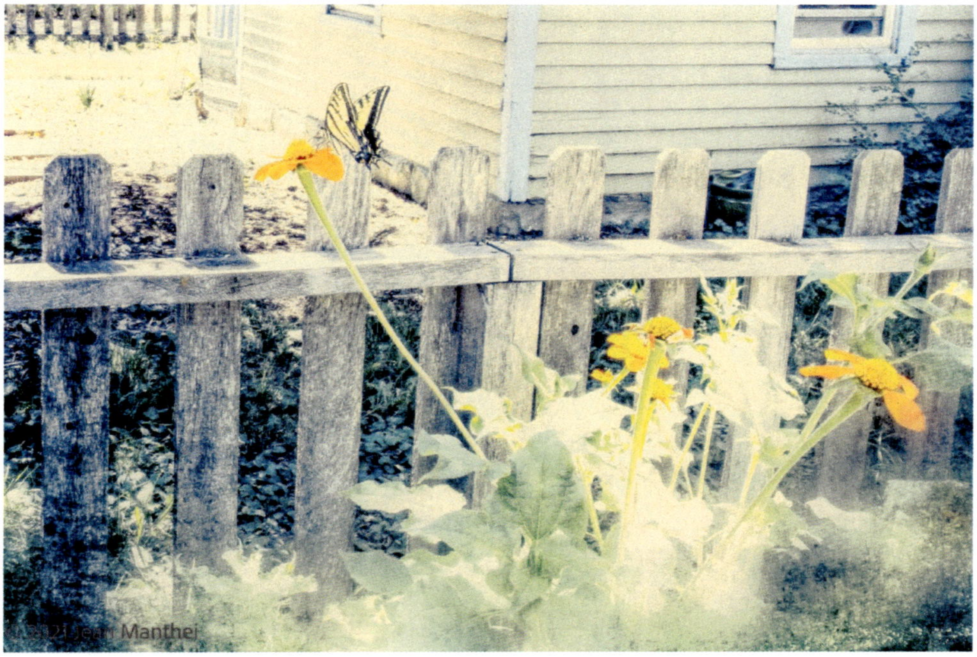
©2021 Jean Manthei

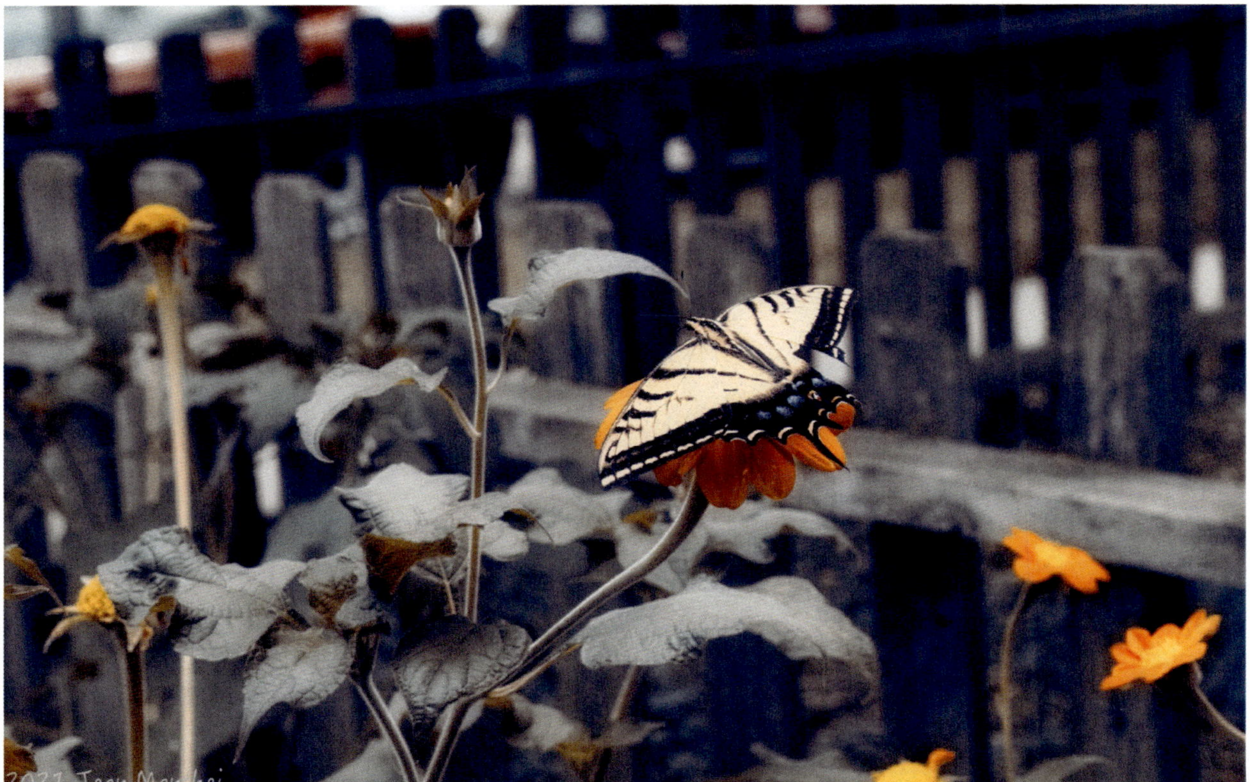
2021 Jean Manthei

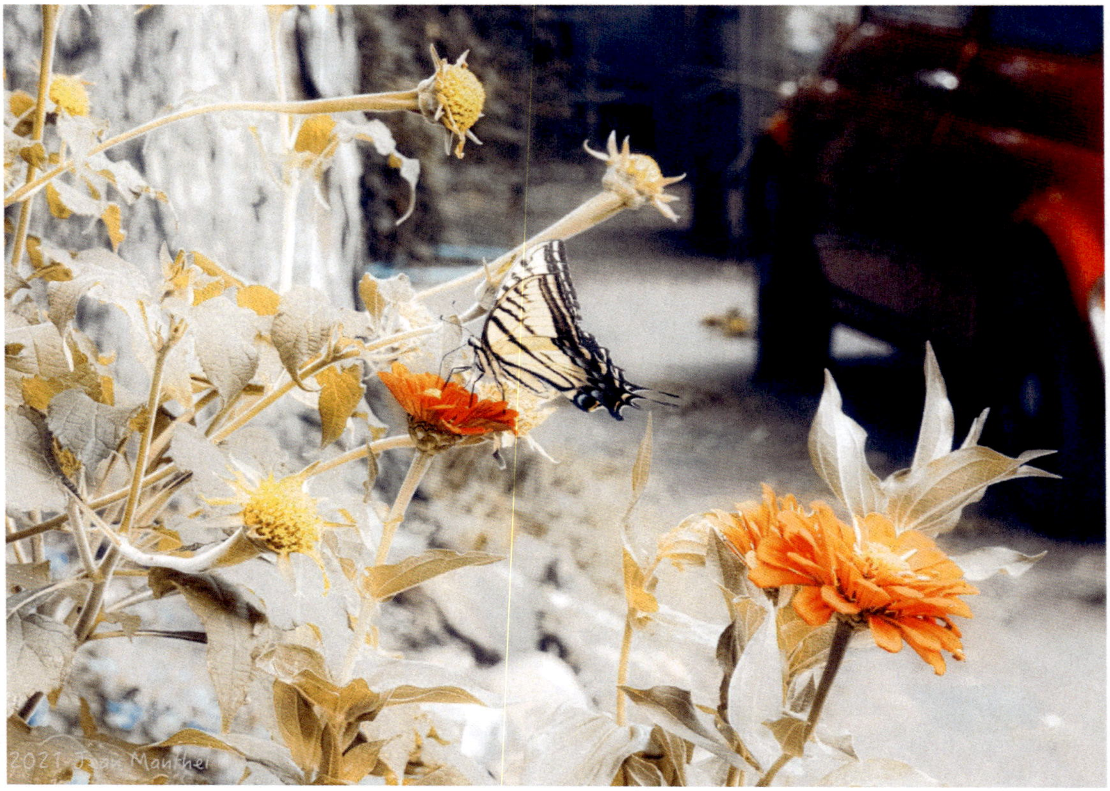

This butterfly I named Corelli in 2021. I've found butterflies come when they're called like dogs and that they have feelings and little personalities. They respond to the name you give them, and they get offended if you mix them up with other butterflies that look the same.

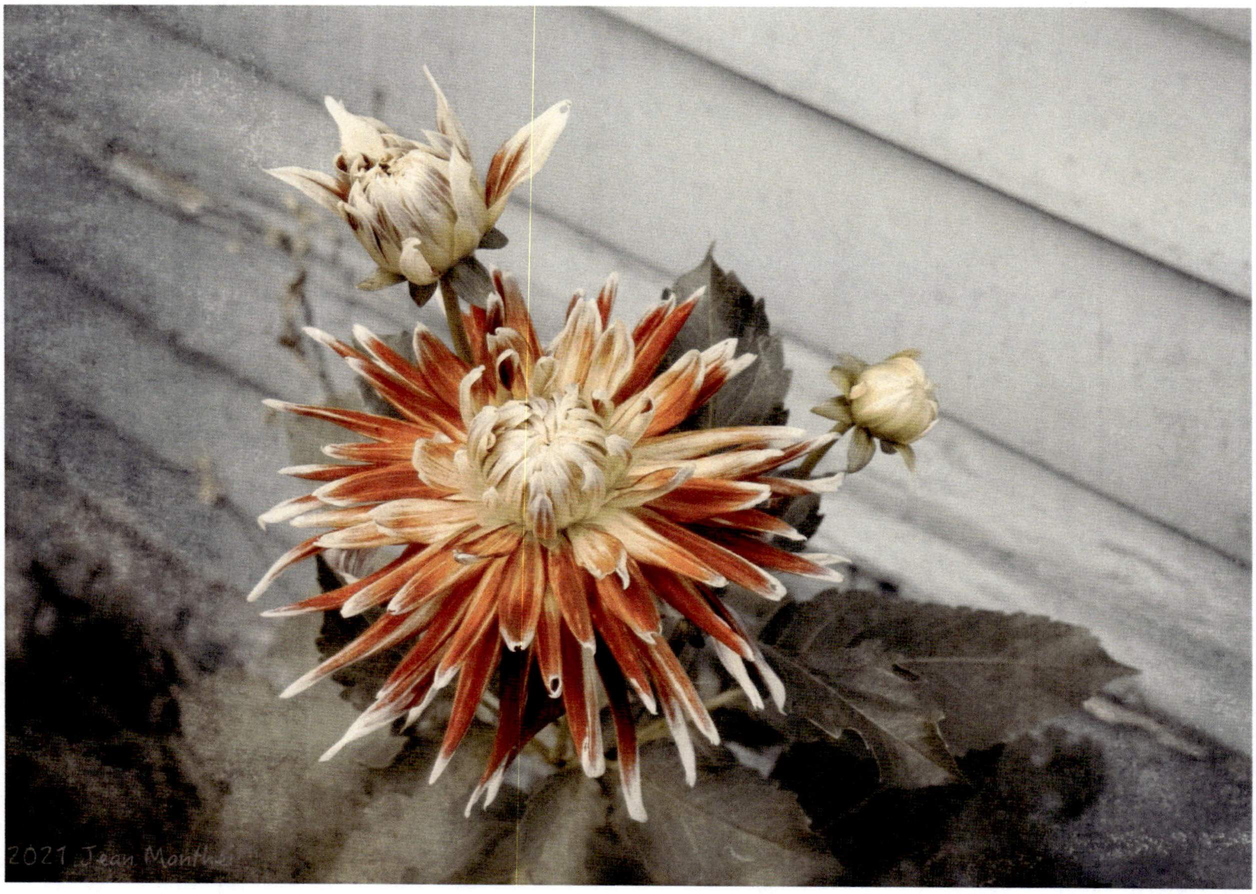
2021 Jean

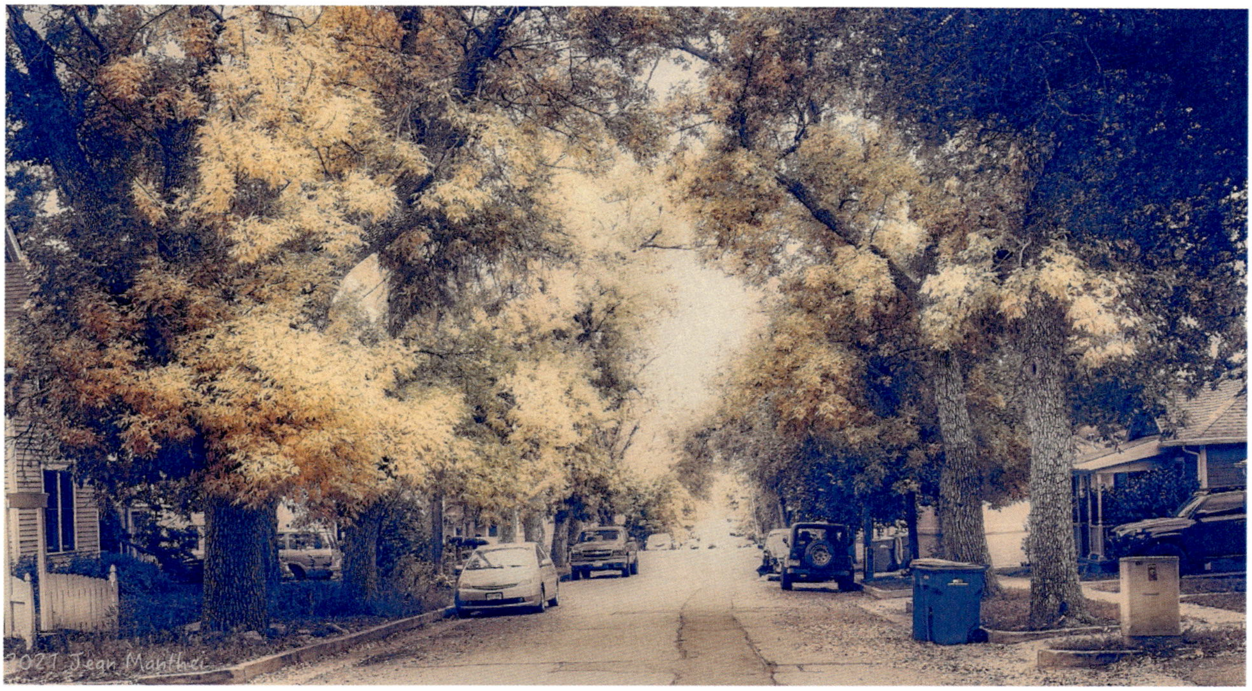
2021 Jean Manthei

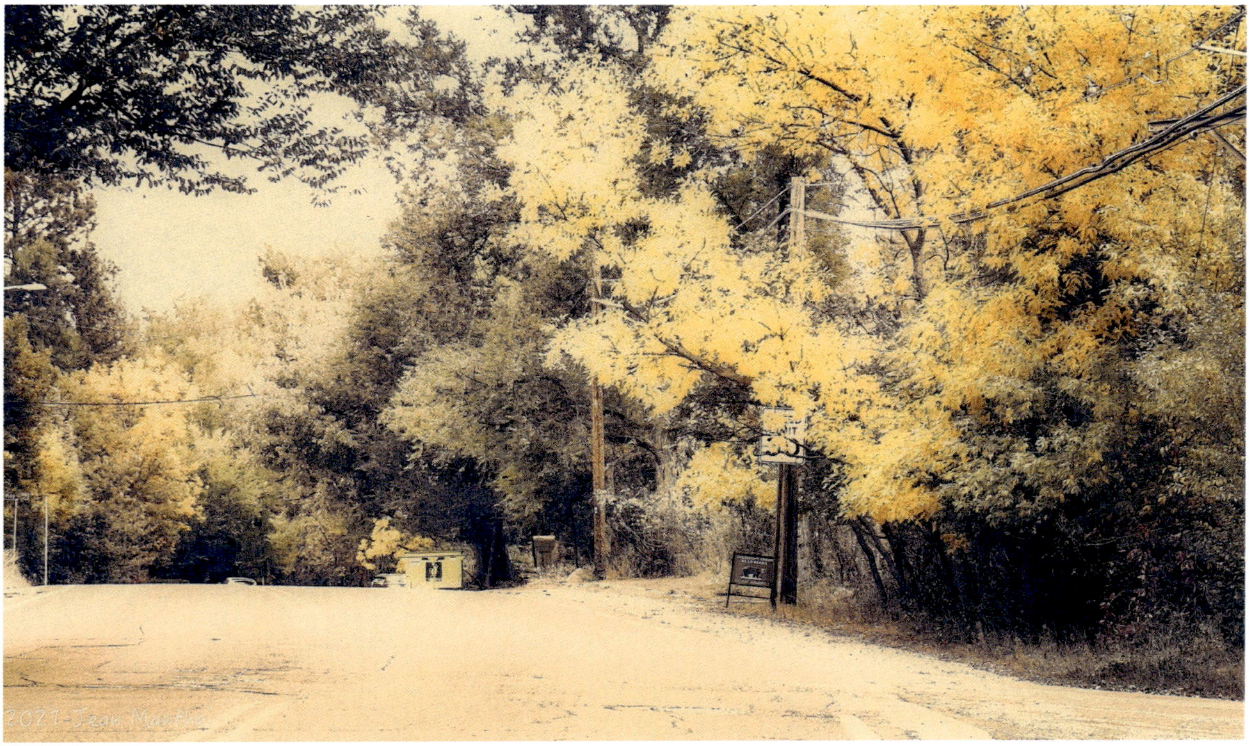

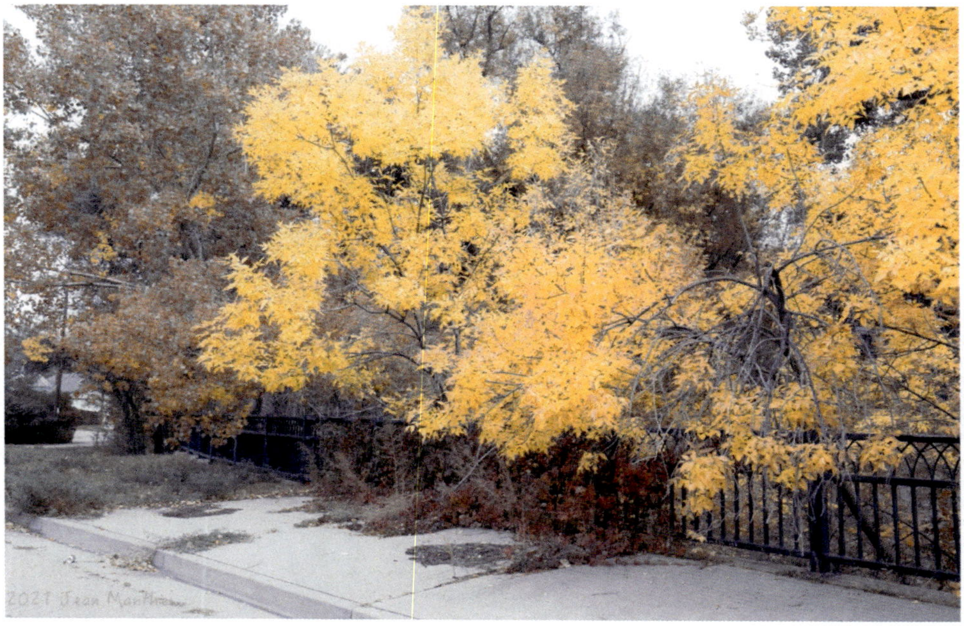

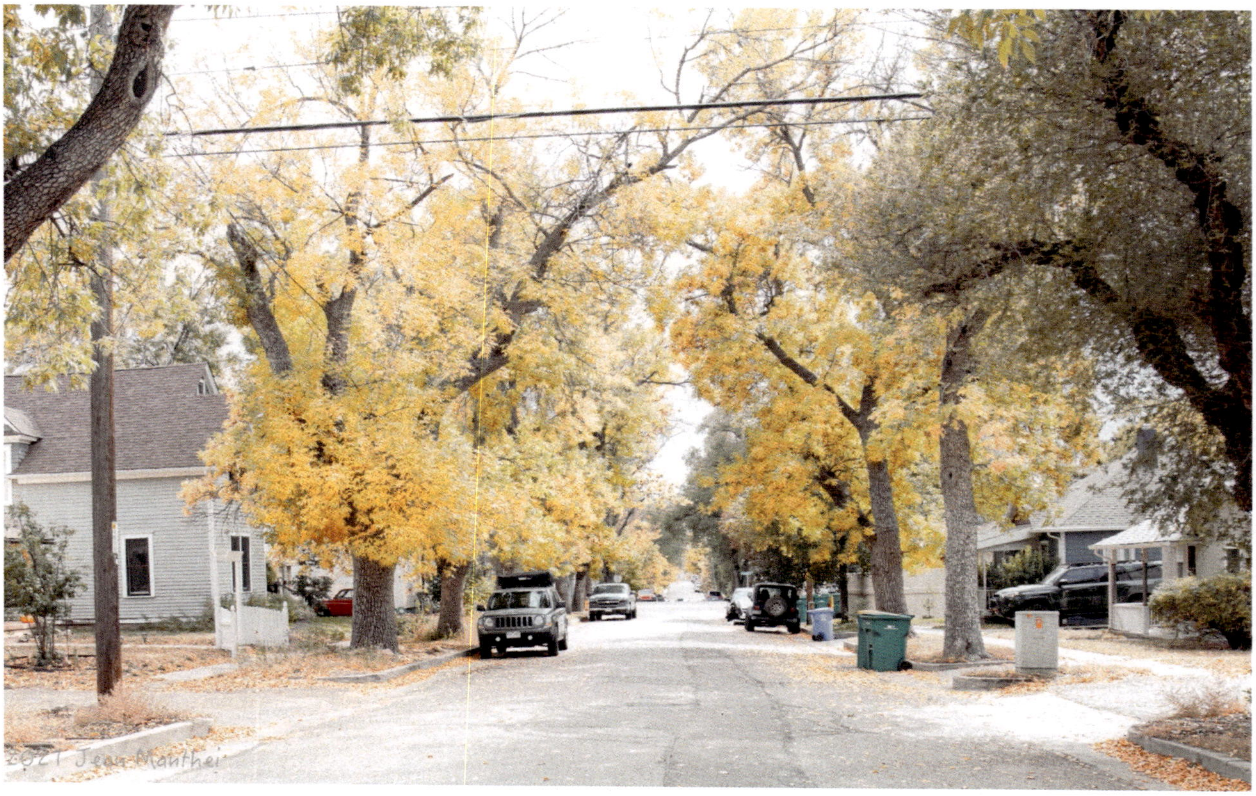
2021 Jean Manthei

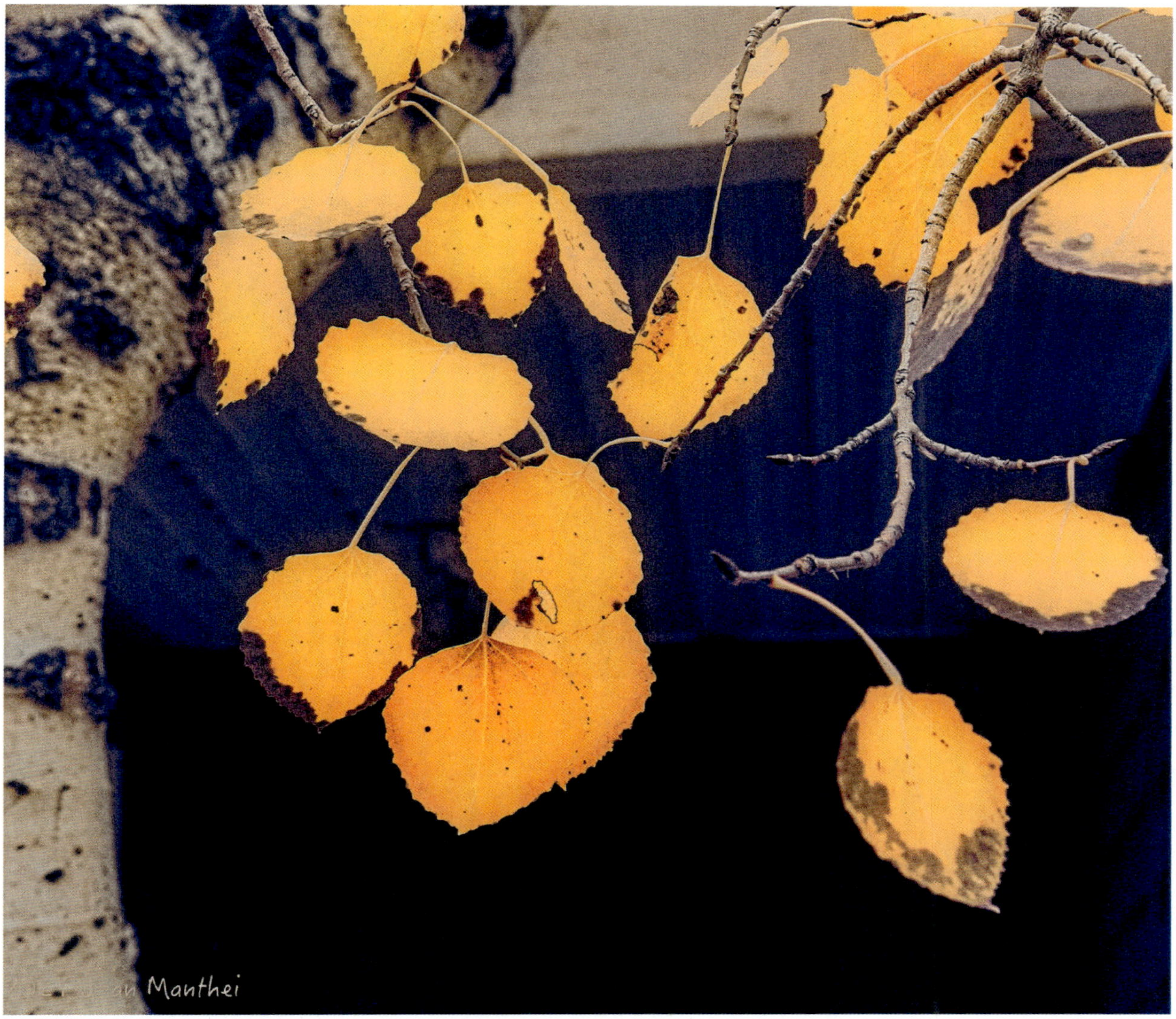
Manthei

© 2019 Jean Manthei

No kidding, I am sure I can think up some more on this topic—it is proving to be interesting. People might really want to know what a schizophrenic could say about photography and the dread disease of schizophrenia because maybe no one gave it one iota of thought before now. And then Igloo (who is the inner child of Jean Manthei) decided there must be a relationship because other artists found relationships of their photography with say Zen and made up all kinds of stuff about that. Then I said, "I know a little something about photography and schizophrenia so could share that."

So, here you have in your hands a practical book on photography and schizophrenia that isn't just some sort of fairytale, but a real book that could eventually be published and find its way to a public library where it could be checked out by people that wanted to hear the latest advances for schizophrenics and this hot little book is it—***Photography and Schizophrenia***—a book for how a real schizophrenic sees the world and writes about it and snaps pictures of it.

© 2022 Jean Manthei

© 2022 Jean Manthei

A lot of "punctum" type pictures here.

Jean Manthei at various ages.
Could you have predicted any sort of schizophrenia or mental illness or tragedy from these photos? Maybe. Maybe not.

The pictures of Jean and her brothers and mom are taken by Ed Manthei. Another picture was done with a cable release by Les Roberts where Jeannie is sitting on his lap at around the age of 7 or 8. He is the father of her best friend in grade school. Some of the pictures at Judson Jean took and some her friends took of her. Her earliest photos at Judson and La Chatelainie are taken with a Kodak Instamatic 104 camera [unless I find my Chatelaine pictures they won't be featured here—found them—but finding them was an issue].

Pictures by Ed Manthei and the one of the local newspaper in West Bend, Wisconsin.

Les Roberts took this picture of the author and himself in 1958.

Pictures of the author, Jean Manthei as a child in the early 1950s by father Ed Manthei.

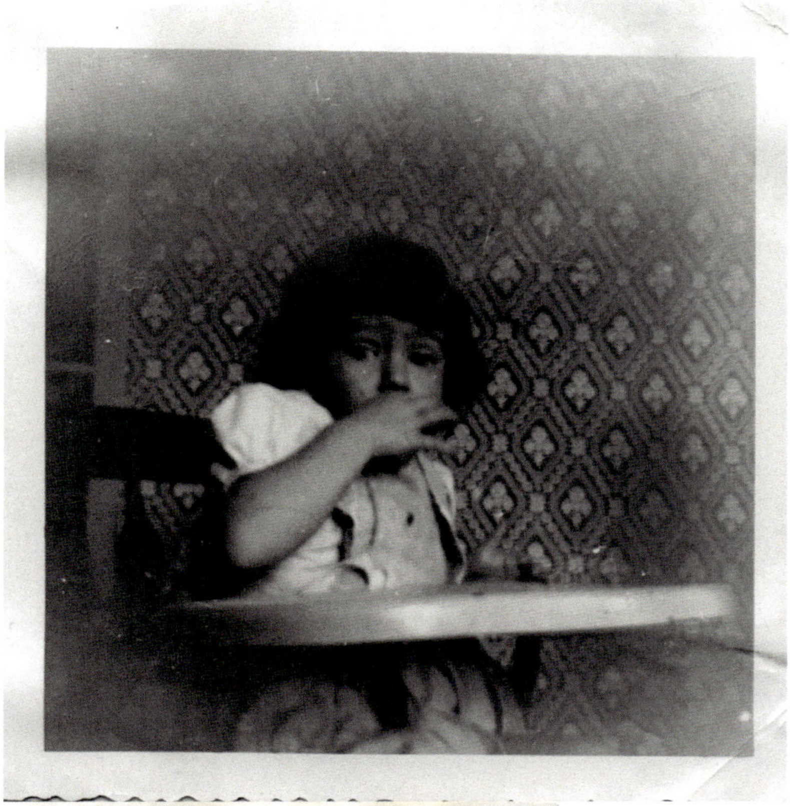

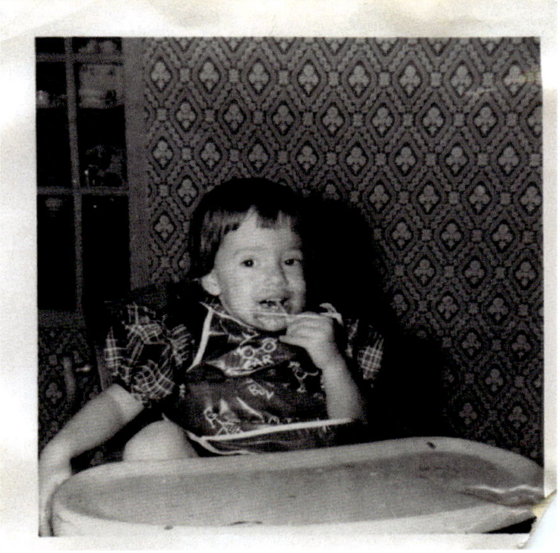

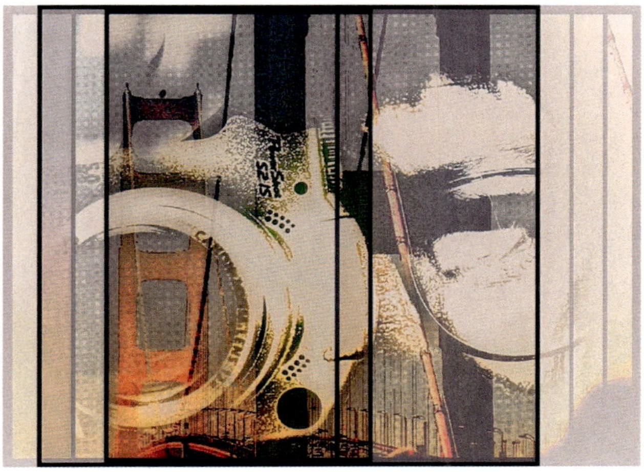

The Dolly's Gym the author wanted at 7 that her dad didn't get her. On her 70th birthday the author got it from eBay.

The next page is shot with a
Kodak Instamatic 104 camera in 1965-1967.
The first is in a photo booth.

On a school bus trip at La Chatelainie in Switzerland in 1967.

Switzerland in 1967.

Judson School in Scottsdale, AZ in 1965.

Jung Frau 1967—Christmas holiday photo.

Lake Neuchatel with sun on the water. 1967. As seen from dorm window. Suisse.

Wengen. 1967. This is outside of Interlocken. Was Christmas holiday.

These pictures are shot with a Canon Rebel T3i and a Canon 70D camera. A few are with the Powershot S5IS.

Coming up in the world.

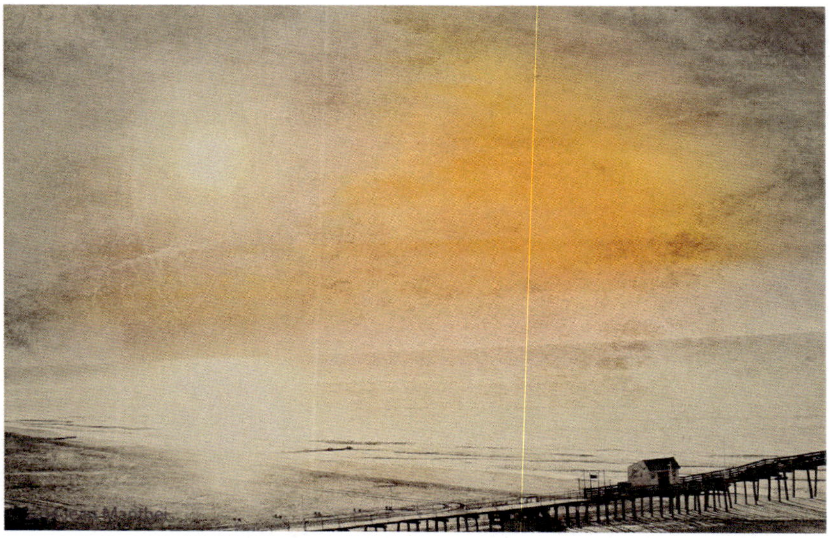

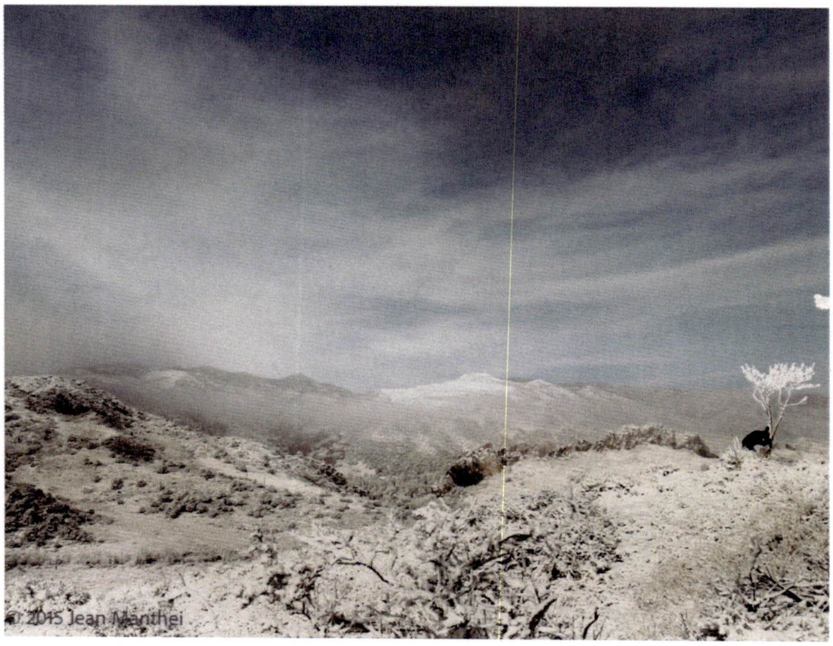

Jean's moon pictures in February and March of 2019 and 2020.

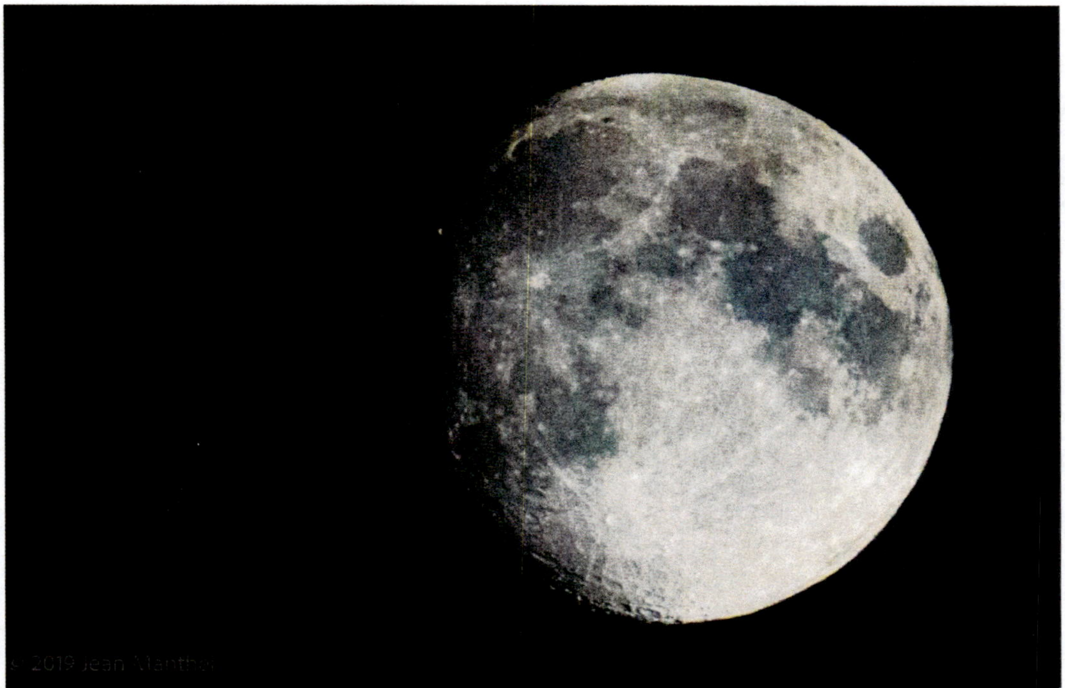

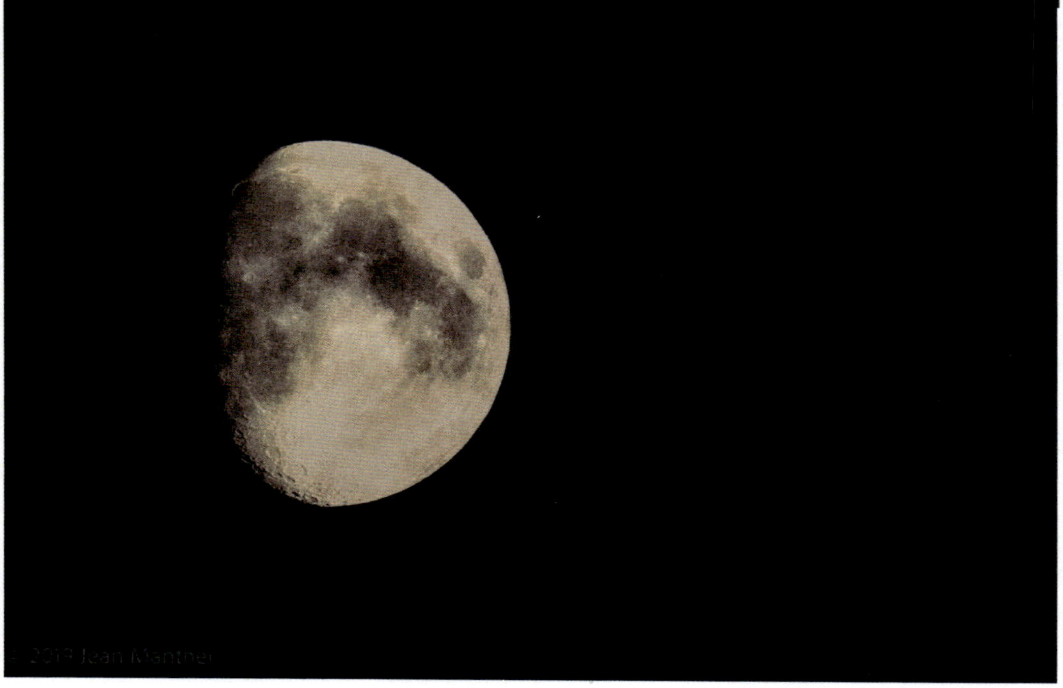

© 2019 Jean Manthei

© 2019 Jean Manthei

© 2019 Jean Manthei

© 2019 Jean Manthei

© 2019 Jean Manthei

© 2019 Jean Manthei

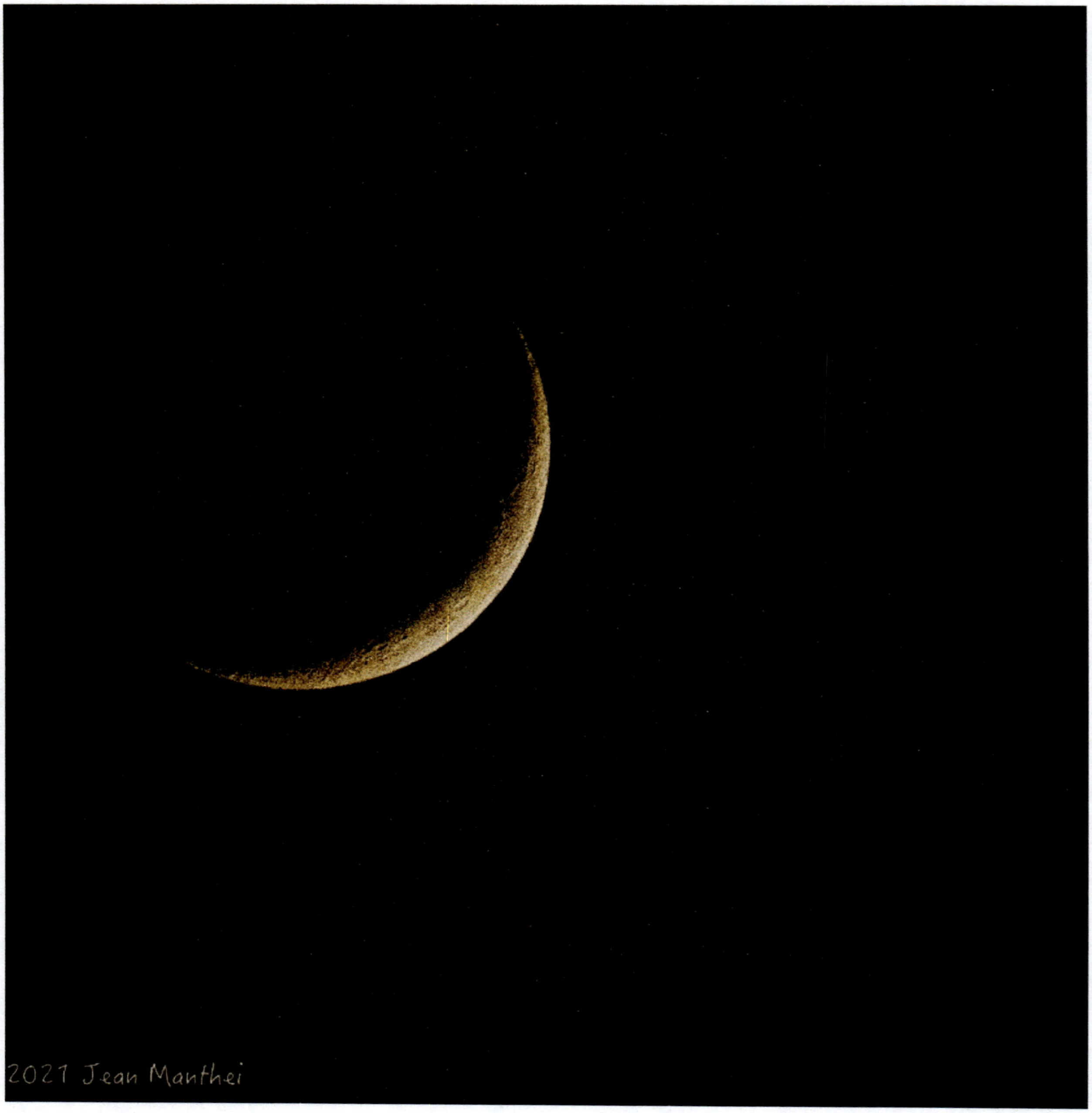
2021 Jean Manthei

© 2019 Jean Manthei

© 2019 Jean Manthei

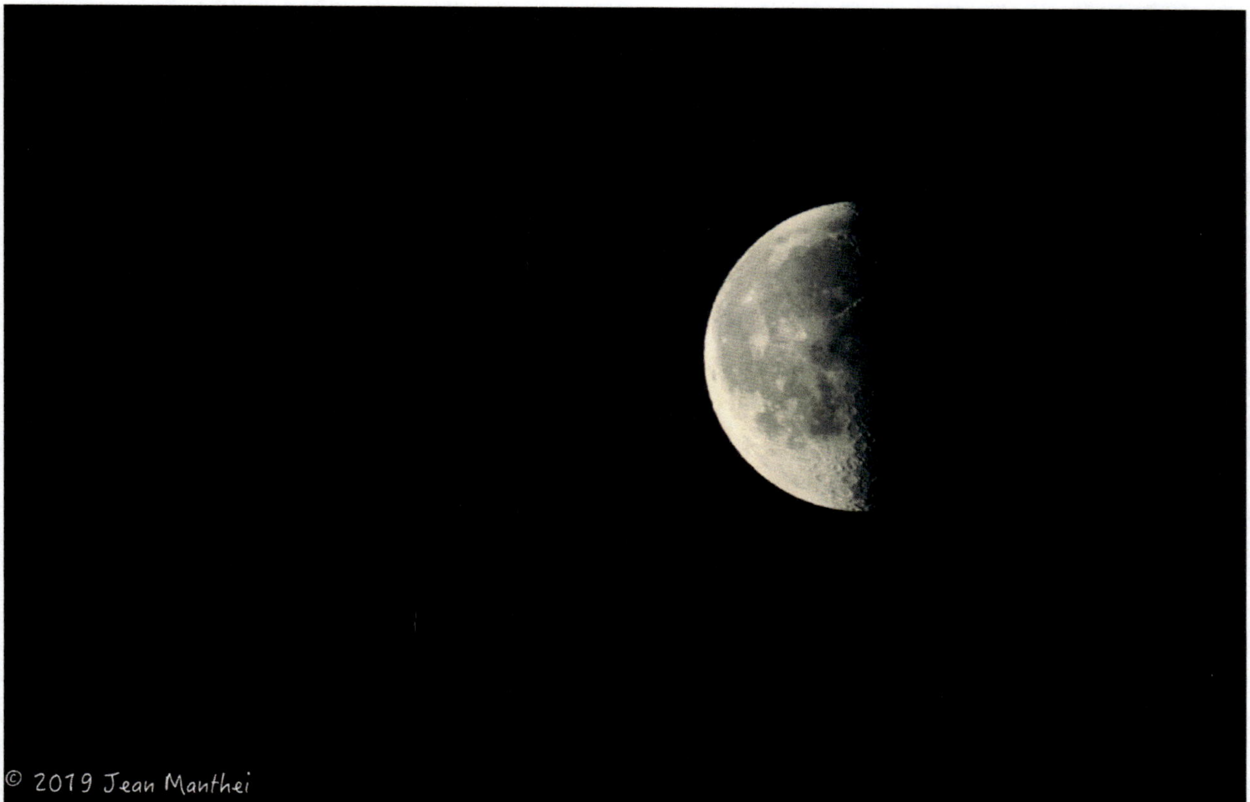
© 2019 Jean Manthei

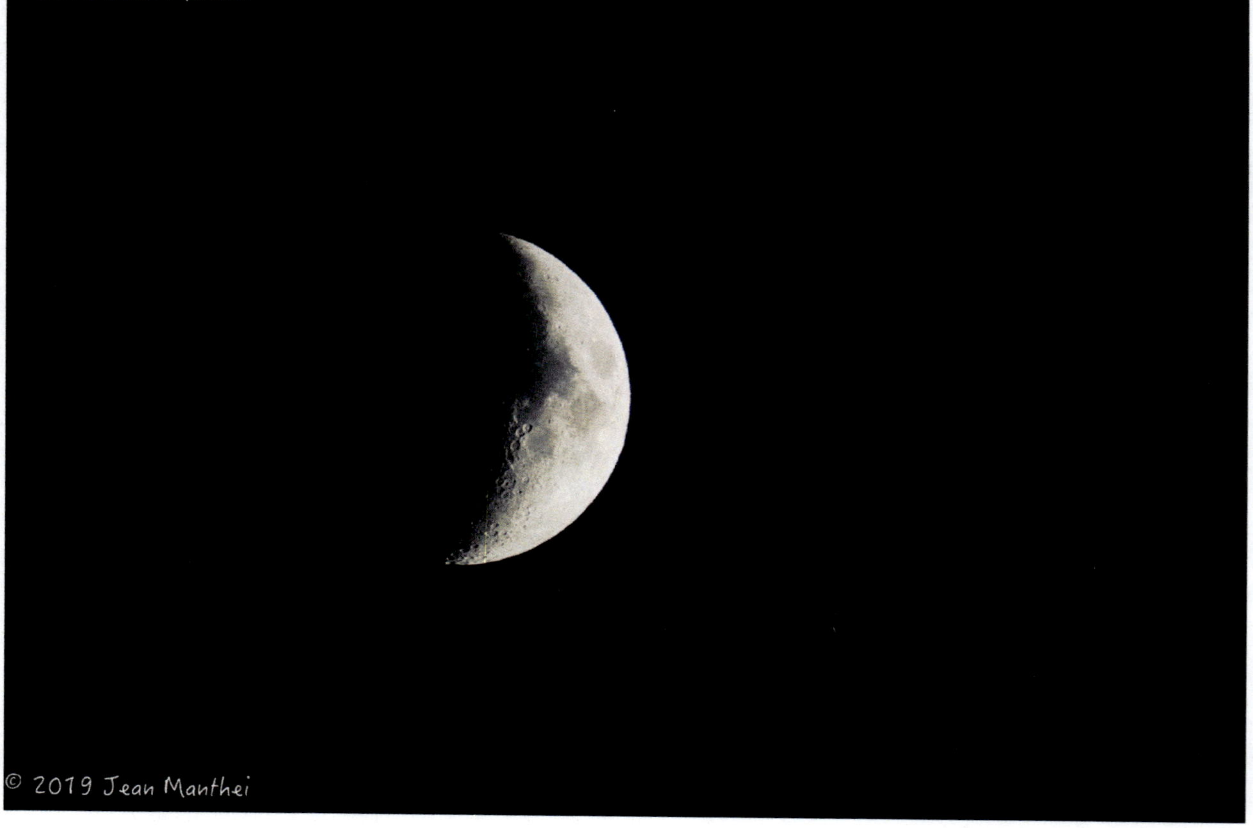
© 2019 Jean Manthei

© 2019 Jean Manthei

2020 Jean Manthei

Those are the dark glasses of the man in the moon.

Sidetracked

Chapter 2

So, since January 2019 I have been reading several books on Zen and photography and **Zen Camera** by David Ulrich, another book by Isenhower, another by Jan Phillips of **God is at Eye Level** and a couple by Stephen Bray who was writing about psychoanalysis and photography. So, this sent me on a journey that was more spiritual related to the camera which may be the missing piece when we're talking about schizophrenia and photography—there could be a spiritual dimension that brings it all together into a more meaningful perspective.

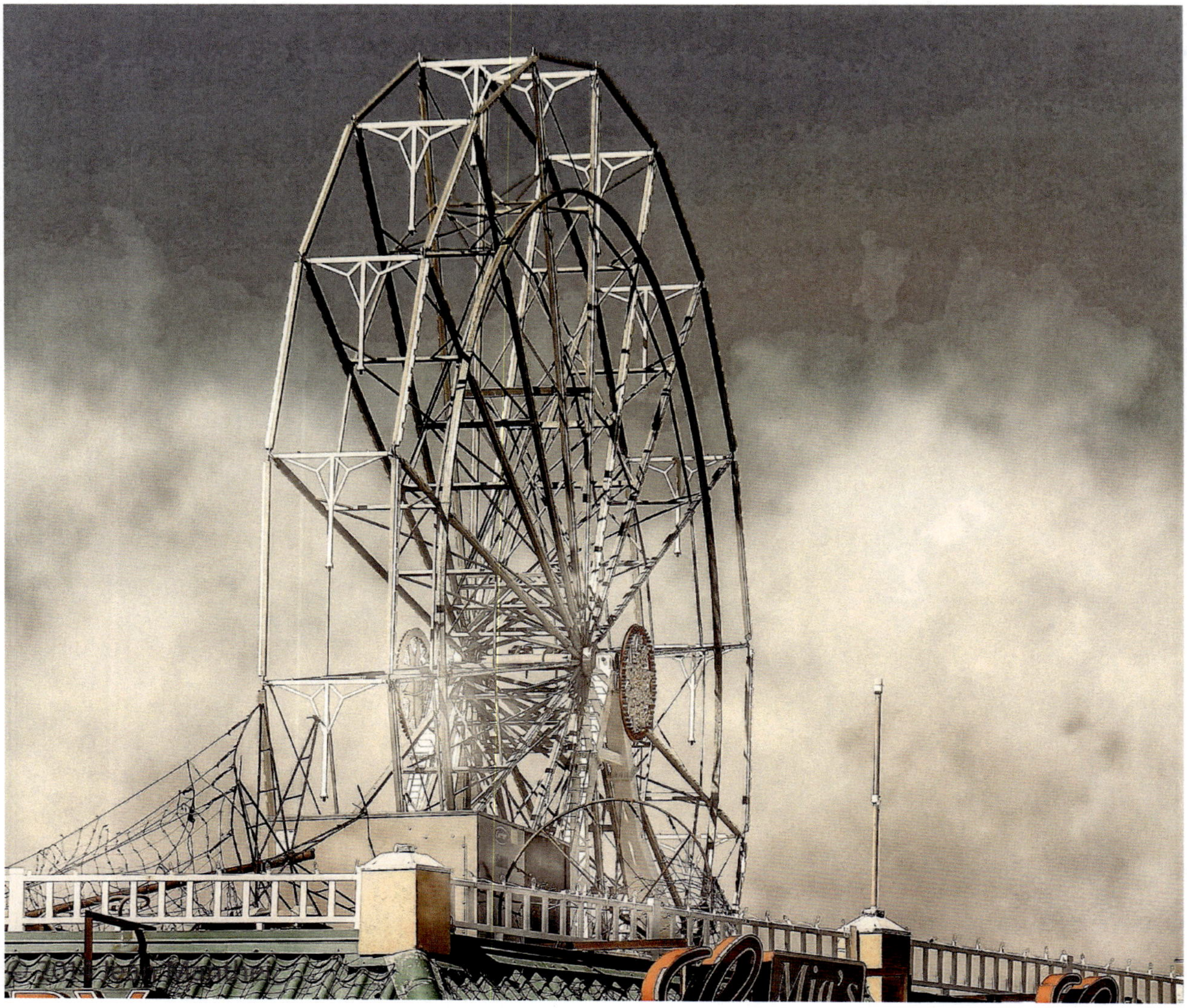
Mia's

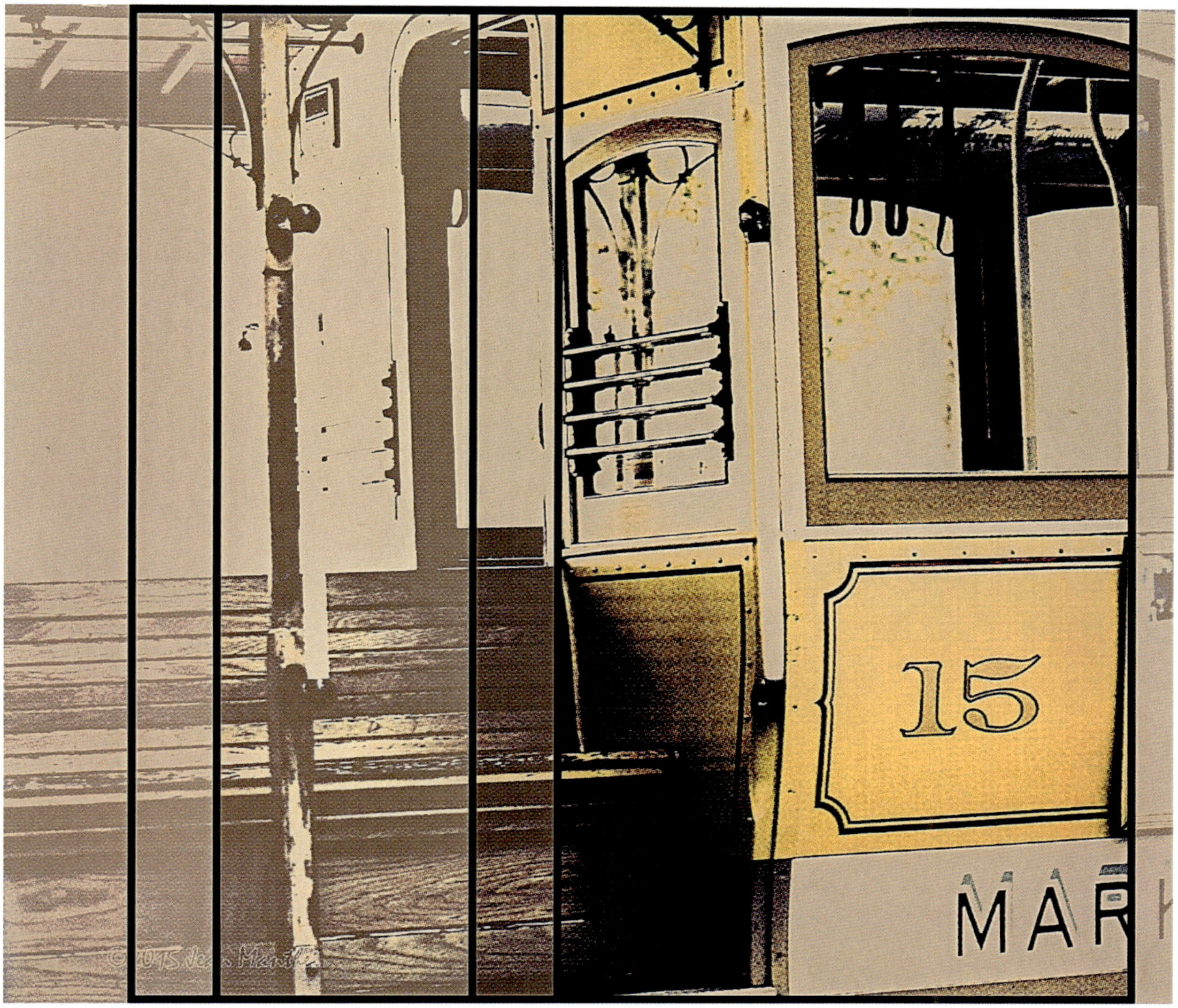
15
MAR

©2014 Jean Manthei

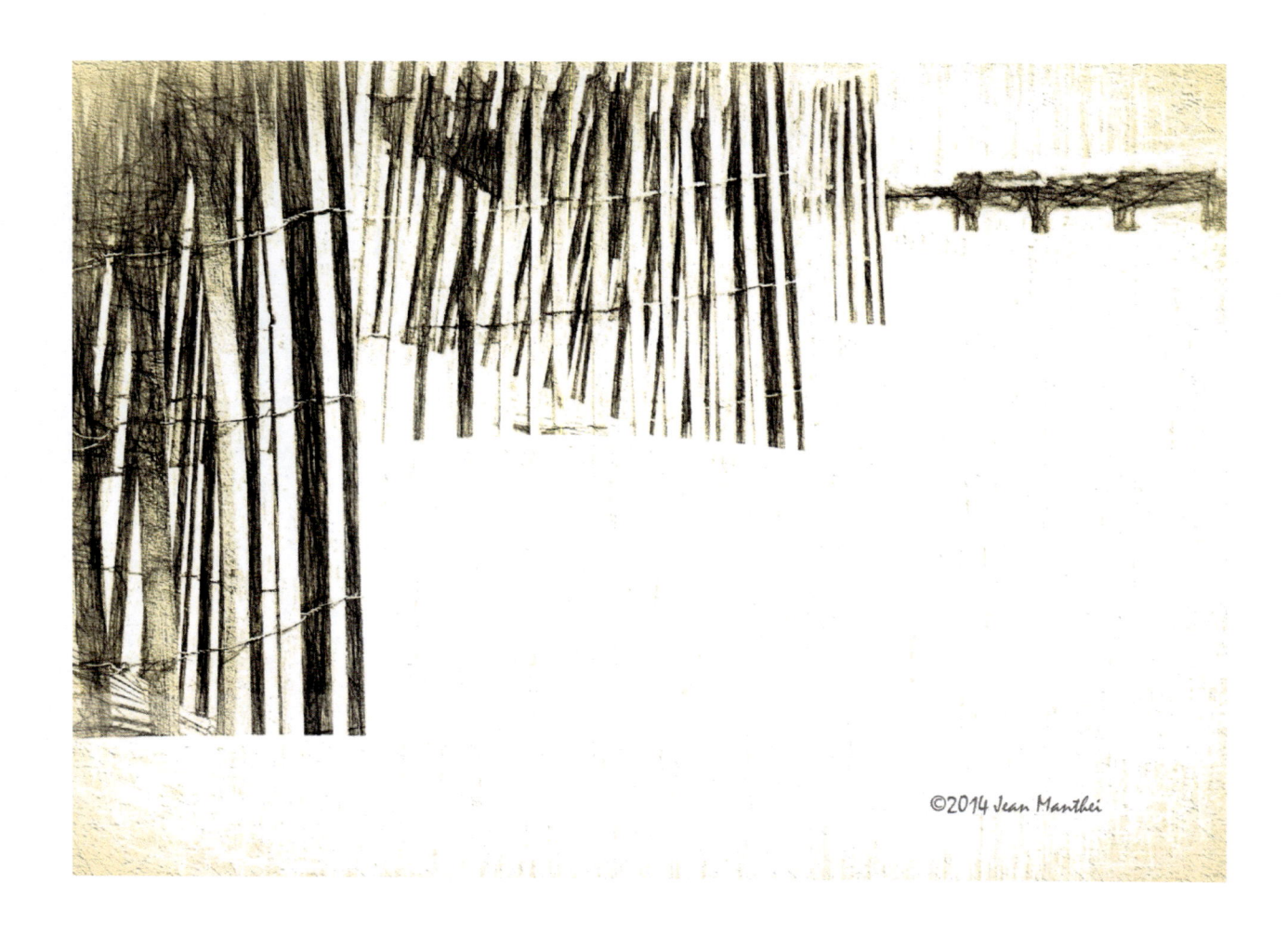

© 2007 Jean Manthei

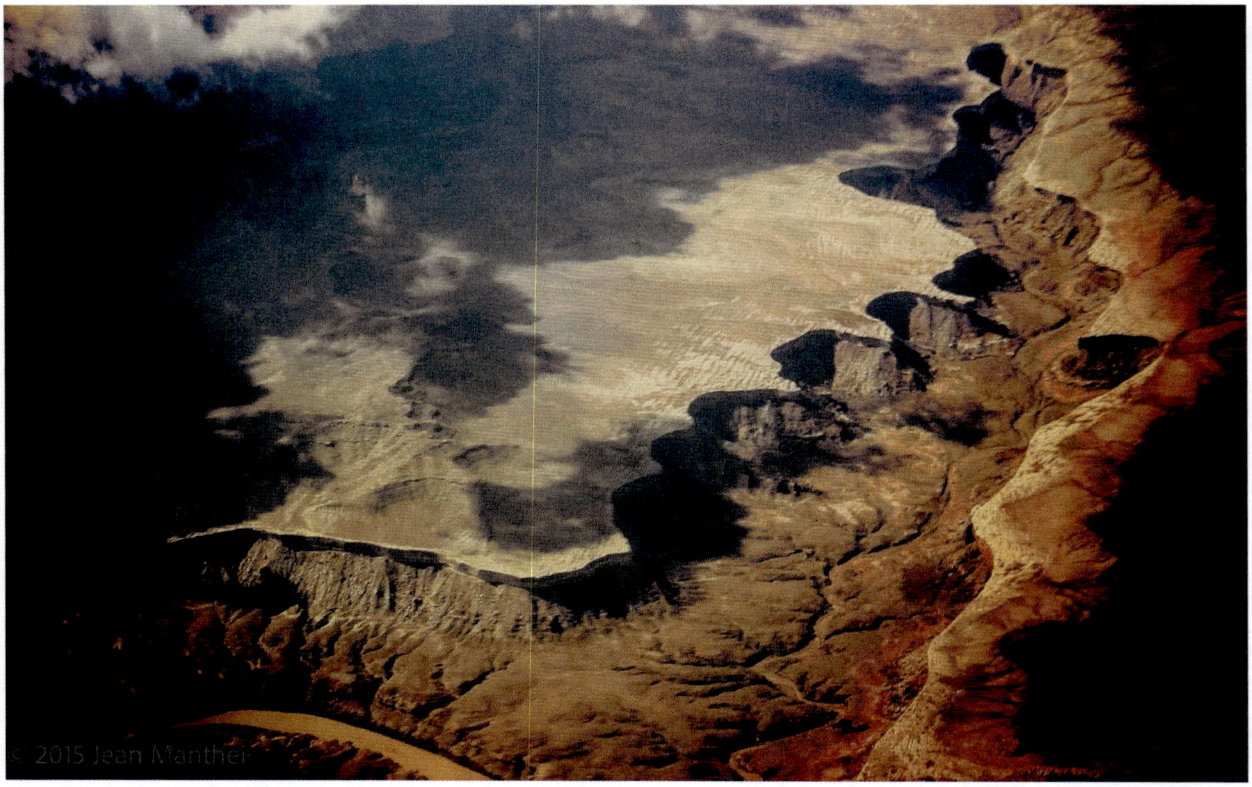
© 2015 Jean Manther

115

© 2007 Jean Manthei

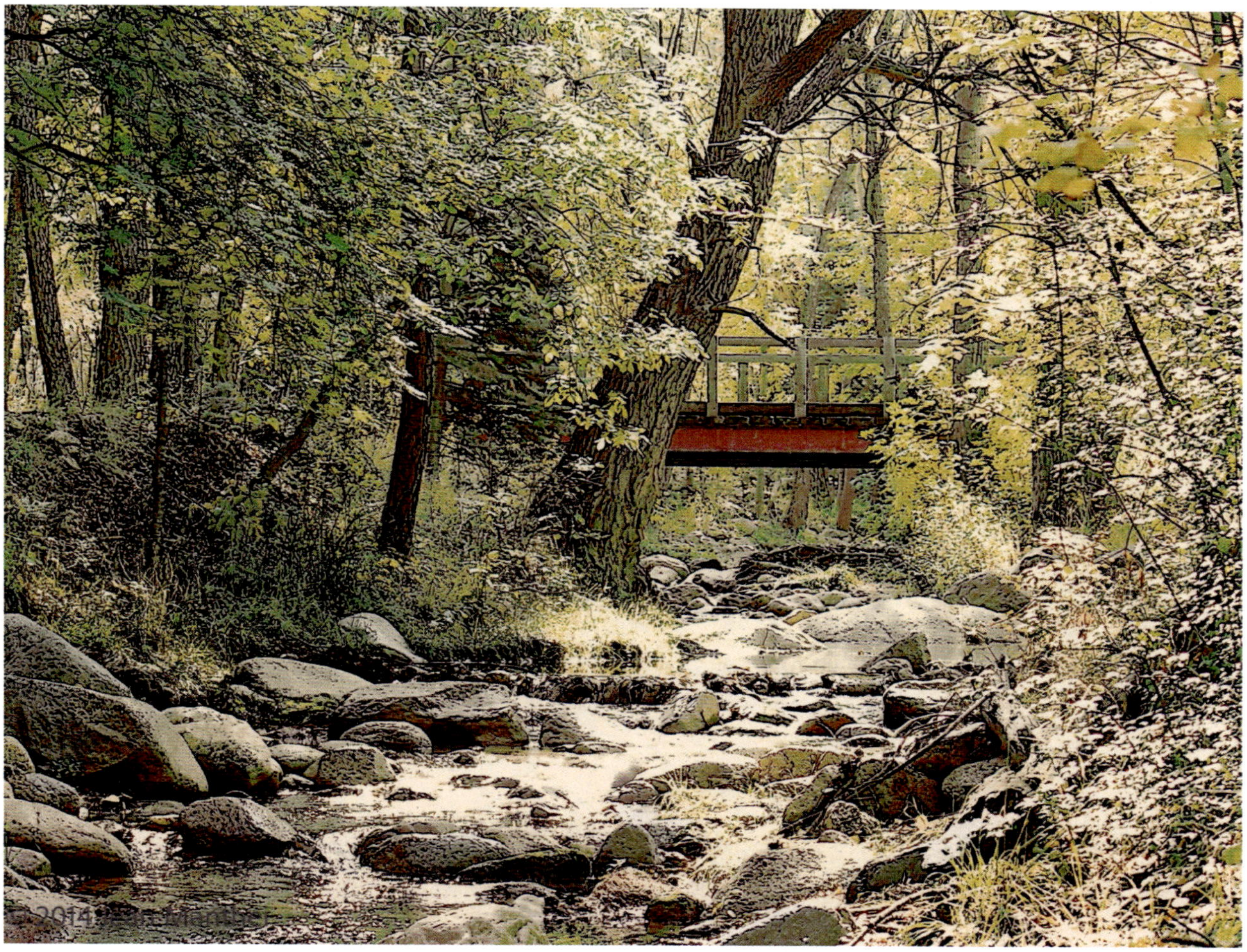

© 2014

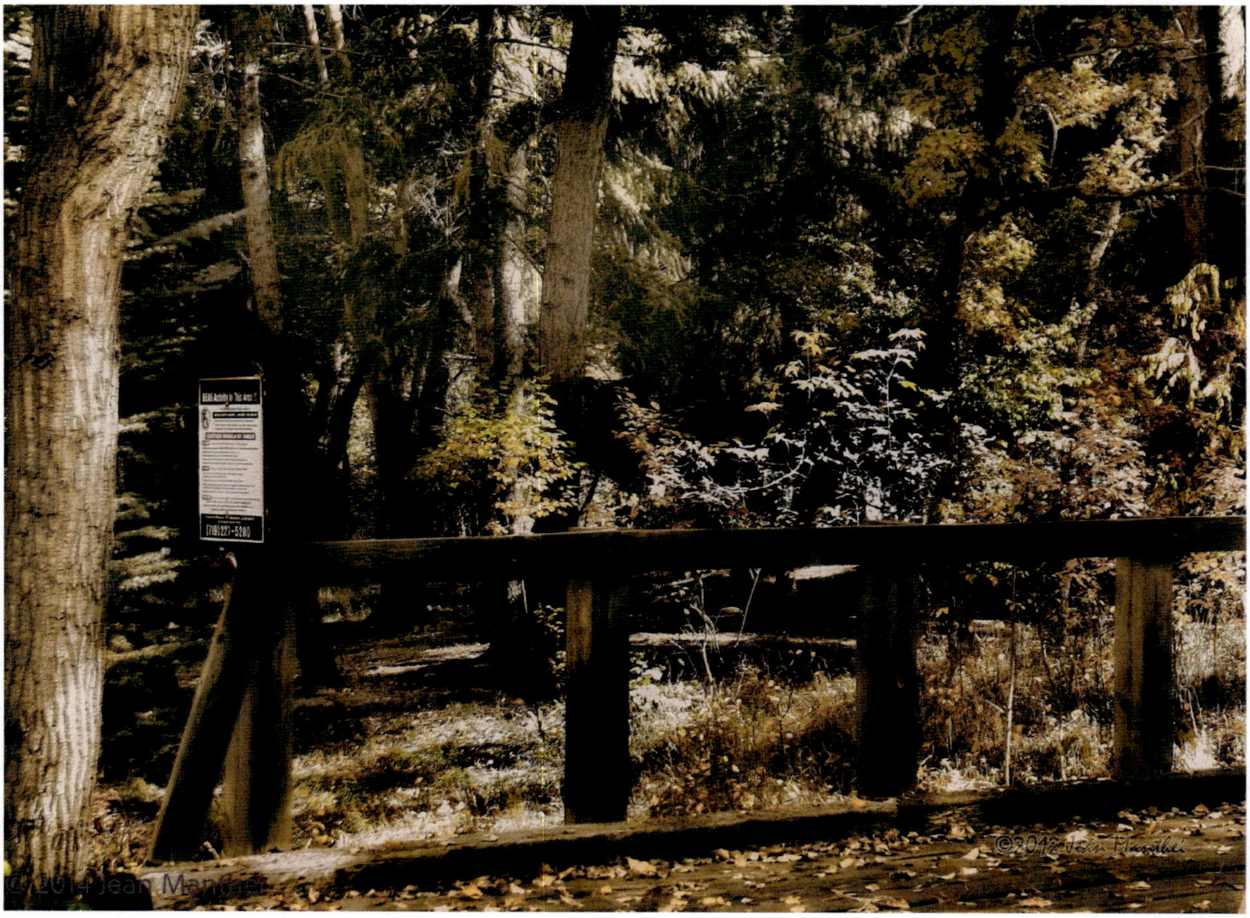

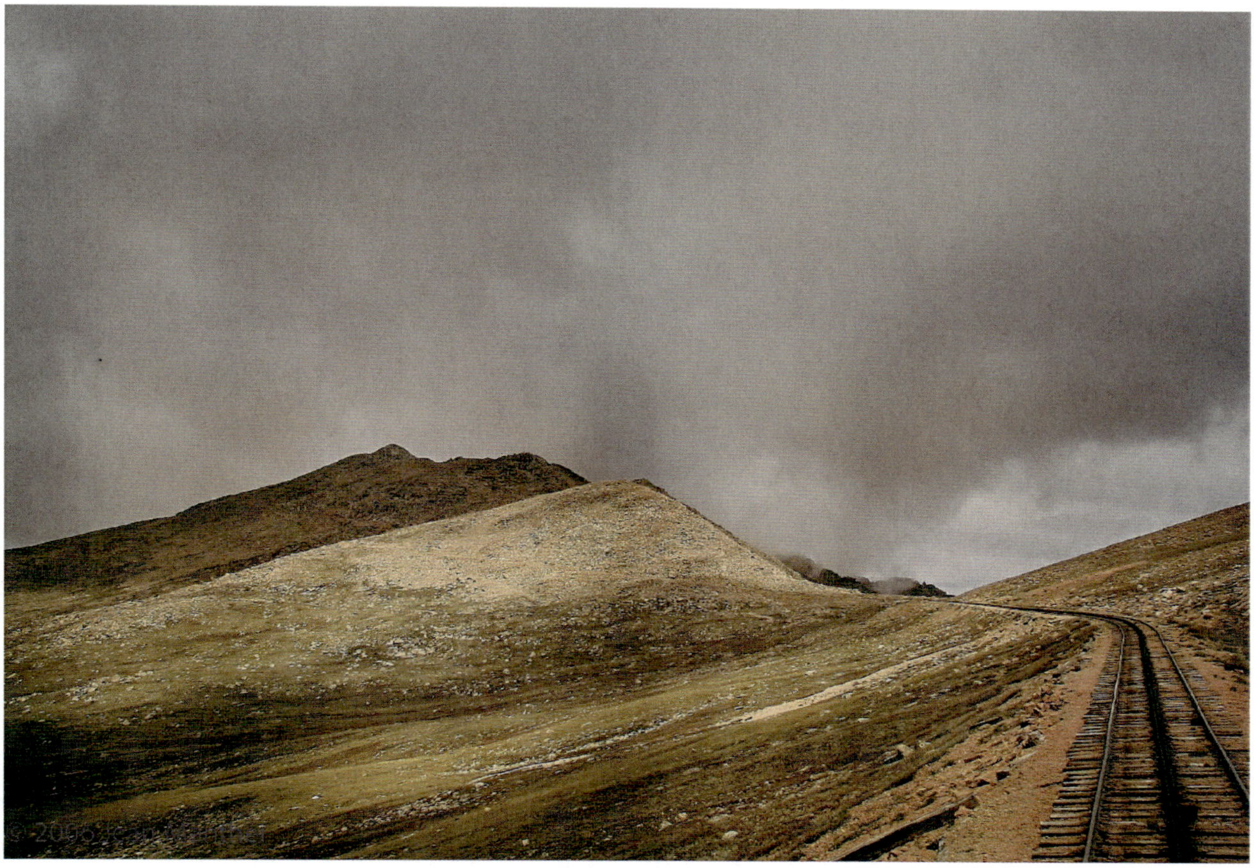

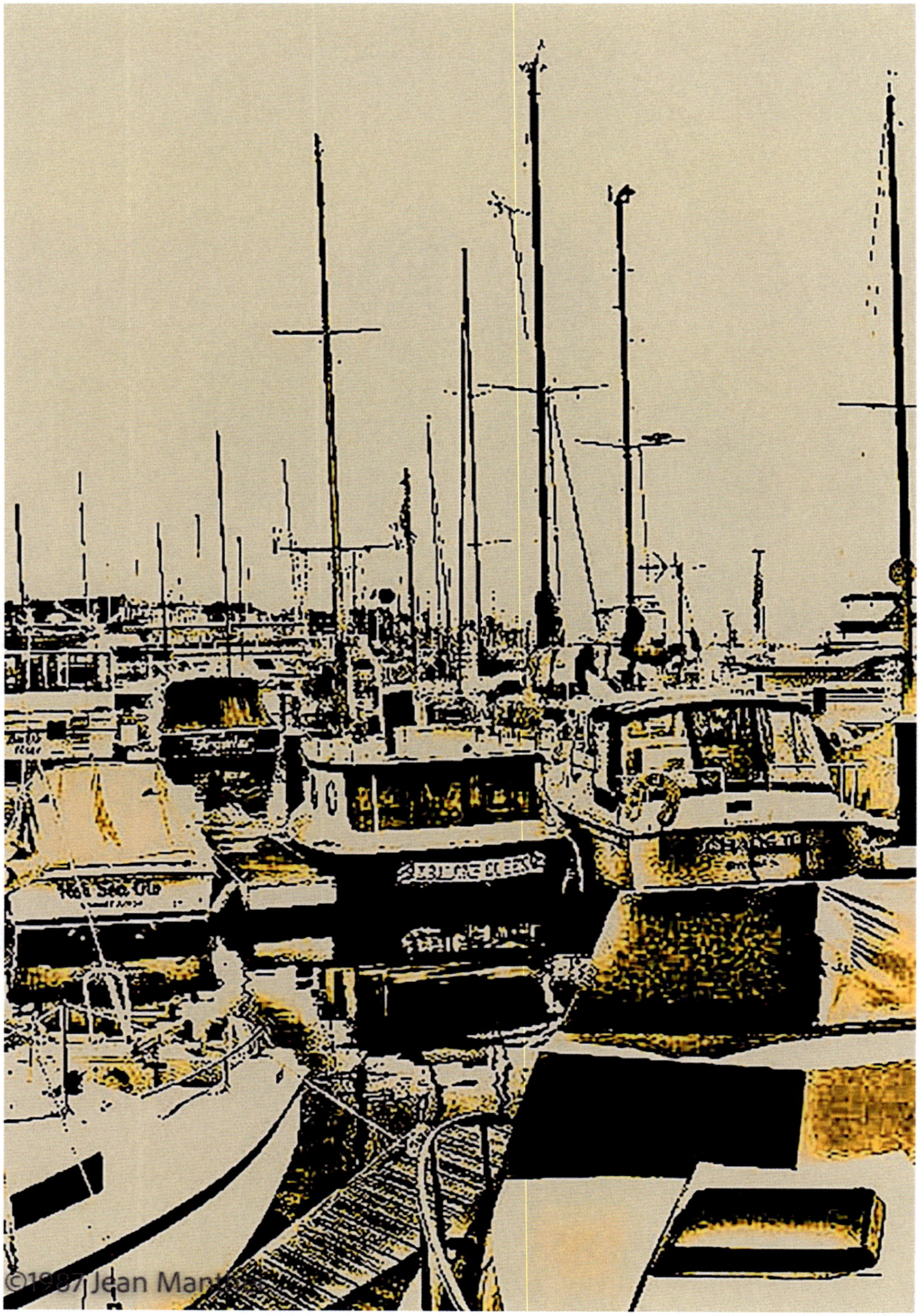

© 2009 Jean Manthei

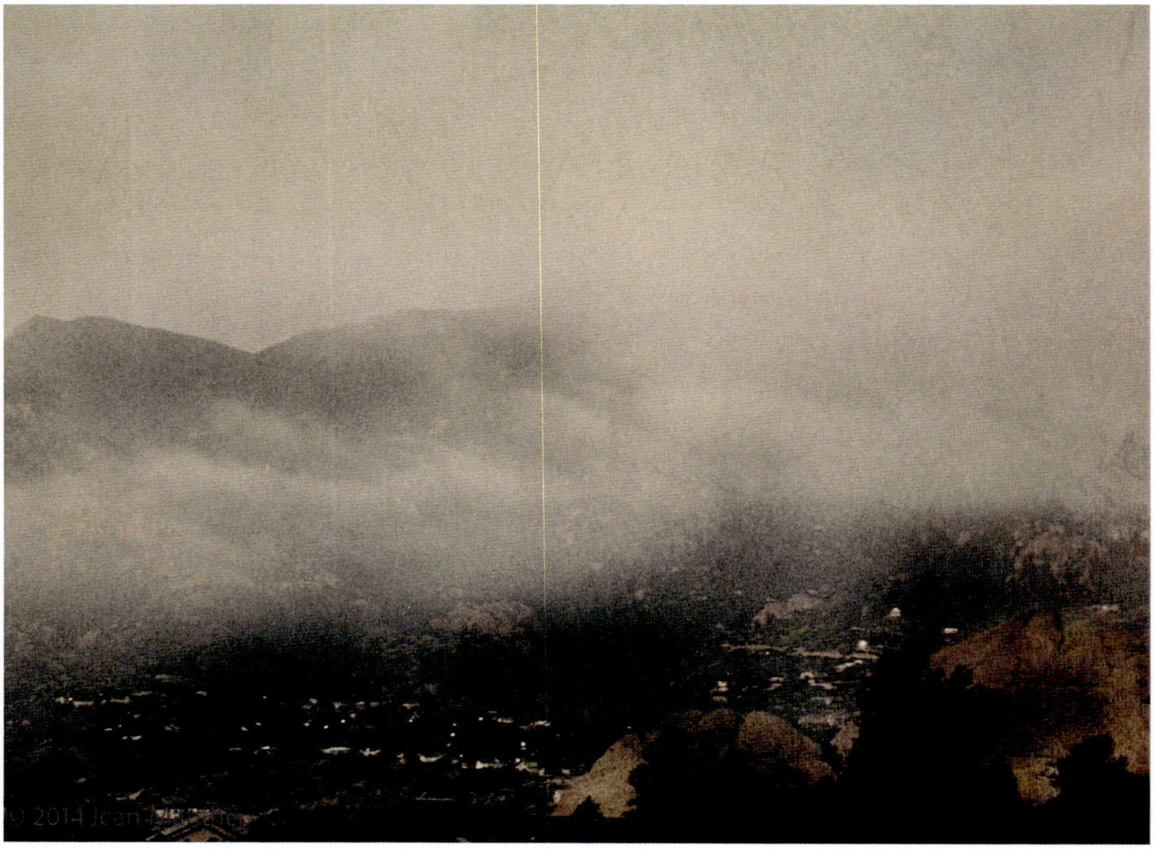
© 2014 Jean

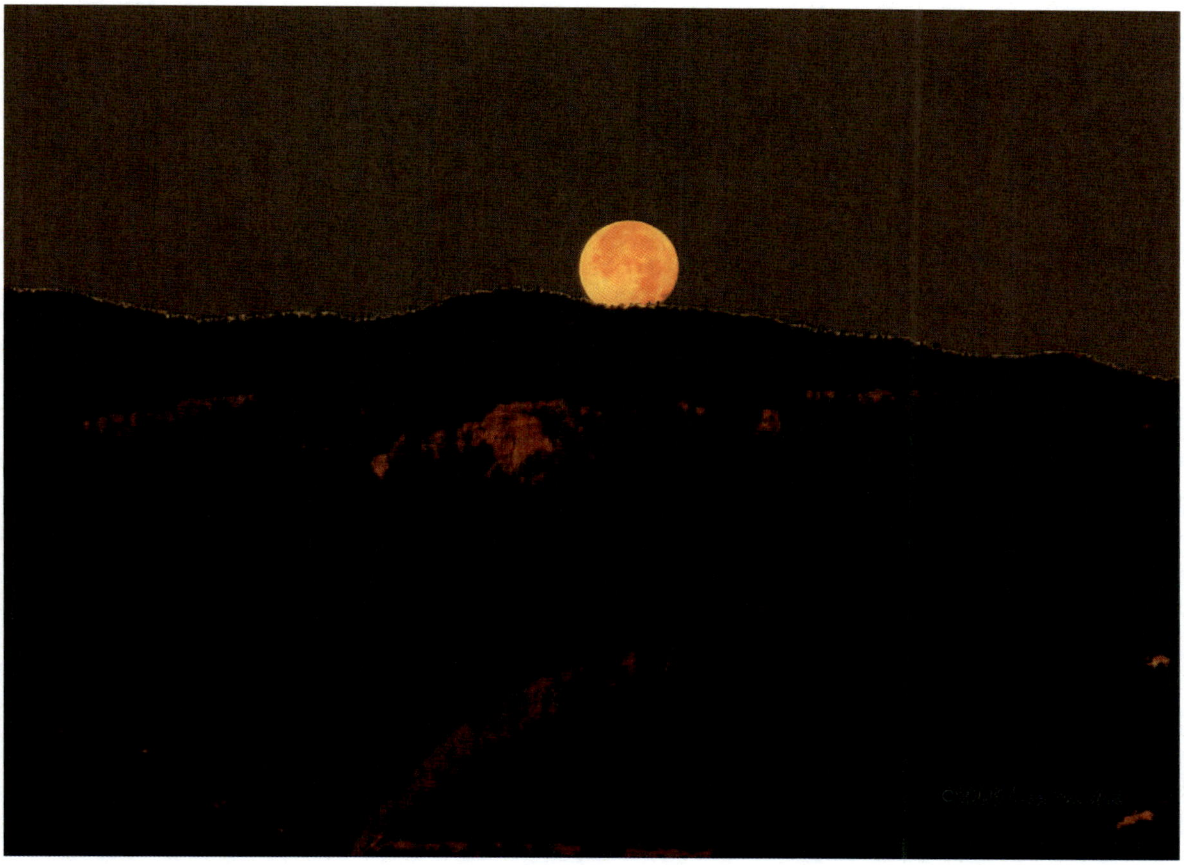

The cuisine that is supposed to give contentment, stimulate the release of endorphins, and give me peace and well-being. Greek salad and croissant. And some yogurt. It's supposed to cure me of schizophrenia and PTSD. Bon appetite.

I had a kid's telescope thing I had ordered from Amazon after the Blood Moon in January 2019 that for my camera was more like an umbilical cord to the books I was writing. The man who had showed me how to use a telescope and a camera suggested a better telescope—a Meade which I got. It came badly dented and I wondered if this wasn't some sort of spiritual sign since I had debted to buy the thing which cost $189. "Pay cash and the thing won't be dented" said the universe. God is much less judgmental.

I kept a spiritual photography journal inspired by Isenhower (Isenhower, 2012). I made 2 8.5x11 front and back covers with spiritual pictures on it with lined pages—waala—I had my first spiritual notebook for photography. I began by asking God what the purpose of these pictures of the moon was other than I just simply liked taking pictures of the moon. But I needed the new telescope—the dented one was replaced with an intact one because I reasoned that I needed to get a bigger picture of the moon—with more detail and more craters.

When I looked at that with more depth and prayer it seemed that I was wanting a bigger picture of the moon because I was trying to get a bigger and better picture of God or the universe or the Great Spirit and I seemed to have been called to take a picture of God or the Great Spirit. My inner child and professor thought that this was probably so. In April and May my prayers had been focused on greater pictures of the moon. And maybe it wasn't the presets, software, telescope or moon pictures I was looking for, but more the grace of God and the spiritual peace and well-being of creativity and the blessings I do have. And then there were life and death issues which were the reason I turned my face to space and the universe to begin with. How would I snap a picture of my grief? My psychiatric symptoms were now coming to the surface. How would I take a picture of my anger and pain and PTSD? An empty coffee cup—a pile of rocks? That would not be helpful to convey some sort of pain from voices and people that wanted me dead. How would you take a picture of a civilian "dung" show such as this? But God kept pleasing me with more photos of the moon. I learned I could cheer myself up with them. The dark spots on the moon? Water. A man with sunglasses and his bizarre dog? Look at some of the pictures of the moon—that must be where they get the idea of the Man in the Moon. Who made the dark spots on the moon that represent the sunglasses?

Then one day I saw green leaves and was called to take a picture of budding green leaves and I got them through the handle of a coffee cup with a Native American warrior spearing a buffalo.

Even if you are a spiritually enlightened photog in this and get spirituality and photography down like a fine tooth comb—you still have to chop wood and carry water as the Chinese proverb goes (Ulrich, 2002 and 2018). Ulrich mentioned mentioned that proverb and it inspired me. Even though you become an enlightened schizophrenic--you still have to chop wood and carry water.

The way I did that today was to do 7 loads of laundry and finish **Recovery Book for Clinicians** and work on this one.

To be the victim of a lot of hostility and aggression is incompatible, dear reader, with my 60 years of treatment, and a Master's degree in Counseling and Human Services. How would I ask God for a picture of that? I am entirely too disturbed for this.

Then on May 12th a Yellow Tiger Swallow Tail butterfly flew into my yard. We didn't have a day and time of my brother's death in 2014. Because it is the 5th anniversary of Peter's death, I thought the Swallow Tail came on the day of the anniversary of his death. It wasn't appropriate for a Kodak moment.

Then approaching the Blue Moon on the 18th of May I was getting different phases of the moon and some with clouds passing over the moon and then 1 minute video clips plus pictures. I had to be up at different times in the night and had to manage this in after work. There was one moon picture that had a very faint and believable image of my dad who passed away 20 years ago last November. And then there was another face of a religious figure from another country.

I kept praying in my spiritual photography journal and trying to ask God how these pictures would relate to someone else and the purpose they were serving in my life right now.

Sometimes I would have a hard time finding the moon in the telescope because it can be as hard as finding God—you must trust the light. You must trust that the Great Spirit wants to talk to you through a photograph.

On the night before the Blue Moon, I had the thought that the Blue Moon, which is rare, was ushering in a new era—peace for mankind, a literary agent for me and success for my books. It was ushering in hope and protection for my assets and intellectual property and photographic real estate. "Once in a very Blue Moon a schizophrenic writes a book and achieves greatness; once in a very Blue Moon a schizophrenic achieves skills and significant awareness."

Then the promised Blue Moon appeared. And it was big and beautiful, but it was behind some trees and houses so I couldn't really get a good picture of it with the camera. When it got higher up in the sky—it was still the blue moon but smaller. I got a respectable picture. And then the next day I got up and had an email from a literary agent, saying "not for us, but thanks." And I was told by my best friend who is a veteran of NYC that the publishing business is about as hard to break into as the theater industry. A lot of people never make it. After a rare Blue Moon which I thought was ushering in hope for humanity and a literary agent for me I hadn't wanted to hear that feedback from my good friend.

On the second night of the Blue Moon, I thought maybe I would have better luck and went and got permission from Penrose Hospital to bring my telescope out to their flat horizon to get pictures of the moon. Went out there and prayed and had coffee with God and sat for 2 and a half hours waiting for the clouds to lift, but they didn't. So, I was getting all sorts of disheartening messages from the universe—and a week before I had ordered some angel rocks for my word rock bowl and the rock that said "believe" was cracked in half. The BLUE MOON BUST. I was asking myself if I was crazy to be out from 9:30 to 11:30 looking for God in the Blue Moon.

I'm sure to be continued. . .I'm not going to give up and stop believing. I've still got about 10-15 agents I've contacted about my book. I still believe in myself, in God and love.

May 27, 2019

Sometimes filled with hopelessness and despair and not wanting to take pictures is the time to take them. I have been agitated and depressed for months—is it part of my illness or approaching retirement? Later I learned it is the anniversary this month of the death of my mom and my brother Peter. And then in July the anniversary of my other brother Carl.

Engage in magical thinking about finding an agent. What kind of picture would convey magical thinking? The moon, GRFX starry night and fireflies? Maybe that just reinforces magical thinking.

Maybe it's just better to be unconsciously drawn to a photograph. Prayer and meditation get in the way of just doing it. You must stop, meditate, and pray and all that takes time. I've sort of integrated a spiritual presence into my photographic adventures of late. It does reduce symptoms.

June 2, 2019

My schizophrenia takes another downward turn in feeling we were all being annihilated in a holocaust. Then I became morose. What pictures could you snap of such a dark mood?

June 14, 2019

Nothing like a colonoscopy to snap out of a bunch of psychiatric symptoms. I bought a purse on Amazon for $28.89 as an incentive to wake up from the anesthesia. Whatever passed through me in the last few months was a very dark mood.

Have snapped pictures of poppies and Iris. There are 7 dahlias coming up. One looked peaked. Hoping they will lift my spirits as I sit in the Mandala Garden this summer. A reminder not to turn to pain meds for pain.

As I am sitting here in this peaceful garden, I am wondering why I went to 60 years of treatment and all this school. I shouldn't have to put up with all this hateful ill will from others, the voices, and the streets. [It becomes 60 years of treatment in 2023].

Have my fountain which is restful well-being. Have Baroque music. Have many presets and profiles to add to the photos I've gotten. They lift my spirits and delight me with hope and well-being that might uplift others someday.

Age 10 with a
Camera

Chapter 3

What really caused me to pick up a camera in 1961? As a child and teenager, I was trying to capture exciting moments with friends and record travels. I had a little Brownie camera that I brought to a family reunion in Texas when I was 11. I didn't know any of these people and it was blazing hot in the sun. I remember thinking I wanted to take some good pictures that didn't look like ordinary family pictures. I didn't think this group or this landscape would lend itself to anything interesting—even in my 6th grade mind. The deepest part of me had no words was looking for something artistic. As I got older and went away to school, I wanted to be seen as a responsible, existential writer and photographer. When all those dreams were broken, and I found myself in college having to go to therapy to just cope with the everyday attacks and assaults on my fragile ego. The only real people who loved and cared about me were my parents that I minimized at the time. And then the dogs I would later come to know and love.

As I went to therapy again, I forgot myself a little and began indeed have something to say. I wrote a short-story and it was featured in Lawrence Ferlinghetti's bookstore City Lights in North Beach in San Francisco. My first book **On Gratitude** was my first success at the age of 60. It hardly sold any books, so it wasn't a success in that way—it was a success because it came from the heart and I wrote what I knew about quitting a 39 year tobacco addiction to nicotine. I had to give up beliefs of being the genius playwright with cigarette and espresso in my hand. I thought of my book as a success because of recovery depth and gratitude.

Photography,
Schizophrenia and
Healing

Chapter 4

Are these chapters too short? No, they're about right. I don't like authors that go on and on with their metaphors and sophistry.

With photography and schizophrenia—maybe the healing that occurs when one forgets oneself and just snaps pictures without analyzing and without trying to achieve anything. Just letting creativity take you into your depths to heal a broken spirit and PTSD and the psychotic moments and past trauma (and maybe where the spirituality comes in). You trust God first and then yourself to allow the camera to take you to a new level of awareness and well-being. That possibly in that trust of something greater that we form new relationships with ourselves and a God of our understanding and in so doing the healing takes place. The soul of healing is in trusting a higher power to guide you to higher levels of awareness in coping with illness and tragedy and developing greater bonds of peace to impact someone outside yourself who hurts or is broken and needs comfort or your grace and wisdom either with your lens, writing or your interpretation or all three. Some entries I wrote in my spiritual photography journal on June 10, 2019:

"I was thinking of how I'd take a picture to work with these symptoms of schizophrenia. Point at the sun and start snapping pictures."

On June 16, 2019, I wrote some more:

"Yesterday I came home from work, and I felt a mixture of anxiety, fear and agitation and schizophrenia and

PTSD, emotional pain, and lack of well-being. I don't know I'd want to snap a picture of anything that represented those feelings." I went on to say: "I would rather take a picture of the fountain or a butterfly— something peaceful to calm me down rather than something that creates stress."

And then I say "when I take pictures and am in post-production I'm not naturally thinking about prayer and meditation. To transfer prayer and spirituality into taking pictures will be a long process. The spiritual experience for me seems to be working with photos later, applying presets and cropping. The spiritual peace comes in the finished photo— "peace, contentment, well-being—yes—a photograph with depth."

June 18, 2019

I've had a few better days more recently. Not as agitated or as much PTSD. Yesterday my intuition connected to events in my life where I was nearly killed and some of the hardships later.

June 20, 2019

Bad day. Asked my handyman lawn guy to weed back in early May and he hasn't done that so far after telling me several times that he would. I was looking at 2' weeds. It's hard for me to do so because of the emphysema. My day off was spent trying to find someone who could do that. No luck. Things were destabilizing.

And that was mixed with other thoughts "so this is 60 years of treatment just to be murdered like this?"

I'm going to see if I can turn that frown upside down and have a bagel and some cream cheese and make coffee and sit outside. Snap a picture of the bagel. I wanted to be able to say something brilliant on this topic—photography and schizophrenia is itself a brilliant connection. I can think of nothing except that this schizophrenia is always in the back of mind no matter what I am doing. When I'm counseling, I'll think "I'm schizophrenic and am doing this and I'm making sense." If I'm snapping a picture I think in the back of my mind "I'm schizophrenic and I'm creating something beautiful—every bit as good as a normie photog pro." If I am praying, I think "I'm schizophrenic, but God still hears and answers my prayers." If I'm cuddling with my dog, I think "I'm schizophrenic and my dog still loves and accepts me." When I dress in my unusual clothes I think "I'm schizophrenic, but my clothes convey stability and responsibility and creativity, well-being and comfort." If I try something new, I think "I'm schizophrenic—can I do this? Yes, I can, and I can do all these things through God who strengthens me." In planning a trip for my 70th birthday next year I was going to go on a Rick Steve's European tour. I think "I'm schizophrenic—a schizophrenic in Paris and Italy—am I brave enough to do this?" "Yes, how fantastic."

November 24, 2019

I really didn't know what I wanted to say, but I have a burning desire to just say something. I just can't seem to think of any kind of insight into schizophrenia and photography. Maybe there just isn't any.

What I'd have to write about is my current life and the shards of stability and sanity with this. That maybe my schizophrenia is allowing me to stretch a little and be creative with some of the surreal Adobe Stock images where I placed myself flying the drone in them. They are like dreamscapes—a distorted door, an hour glass in a sand dune. This might be a creative aspect of my illness. I am putting those creations in a Shutterfly photo book and putting some of the dreams I had from journals in the 20th century. It's called ***Dreamscapes.***

I really want to say something about schizophrenia and photography that is new, original, and not said before. What are those needs for originality and greatness? That I am someone and that I matter, that I have talent in my own right and that I have something to contribute. That while I may be schizophrenic and a hero zero, I am respectable in my own right as a counselor and a responsible schizophrenic: "Please don't shoot."

My inner child doesn't like to be treated like a slot machine for a jackpot of creativity and inspiration. If I am to rise to the occasion and say anything of depth or originality it won't be forthcoming if I am disrespectful to myself and treat myself as a slot machine. Igloo would be mad.

I surely must have something substantial I can say about this illness and the wonderful world of photography and pictures and the need to snap pictures and make psychological and emotional and political statements in managing my illness and working through tough issues and feelings and trauma.

I kept waiting for something important to appear out of the unconscious and it is just not forthcoming on this 24th day of November 2019.

What I did was eat dinner and did a 10 minute-meditation in which I emerged laughing.

What I wrote was good. It was like zooming in on a creative moment. Creativity can't be forced—I just have to cast my net into the unconscious and wait for the connection between the idea of schizophrenia and photography to fall into the net. My excitement was not in tune with an insight. The insight might not have caught up to the excitement. I trust my excitement. It's as though it is some preverbal experience, and the words haven't found expression of something I saw or understood in pictures or emotions, but not verbally. So, there Igloo, I am not a pinata. Something is coming from the crawl space of my unconscious, and I will trust that it will be well-timed with the excitement and peace I feel today.

November 25, 2019

It just feels good to take a great picture whether you're schizophrenic, Bi-polar, antisocial, autistic or borderline or normal (normal is not capitalized because it is not considered a disorder or is it?).

Photography is a riveting human experience if you have a good eye and feel for composition and ideas. Diagnosis shouldn't matter.

My picture of Ketu looking at her picture in ***On Gratitude*** with the thought "Ketu is good with schizophrenic authors" was humorous and gratifying to my soul. But the picture spoke of a great bond and love between a schizophrenic and her dog which any kind of love when you have this dread disease of schizophrenia is difficult to establish and maintain. The picture might have been a breakthrough picture for me. For some reason that picture conveys many ideas and levels of communication and understanding, and it is humorous.

It is possible that the therapeutic value it can have if you have schizophrenia or other mental health issues are deep, unconscious breakthroughs like that that process preverbal material and things about your illness and conclusions in regard to say trauma or PTSD and symptoms of one's illness or thinking that previously were speechless metaphors—wordless thoughts and understandings, suddenly now, with a photograph, bigger understandings and connections can be made. And that is where the breakthroughs are possible and new associations are formed.

For the picture of Ketu and the author's book ***On Gratitude***, a dog cannot comprehend that a schizophrenic wrote a book such as this where the picture of her saying "Ketu never turned her back or used domestic violence on me" would be comprehensible to a dog. But the dog's facial expression and her rapt attention and gaze upon the book makes it very believable that the doggie comprehends every word and idea. And that idea is love. The fact that she is so loving to the author obviously made

her good with schizophrenic authors. It is the idea that it takes a very special and unique dog to be good with a high strung, schizophrenic author. In this case it is easy to use one's imagination to get into the playfulness of it all and believe this is obviously the case for the schizophrenic author and her dog. How could it not be otherwise—why this makes perfect sense don't you think? The picture seems to capture this breakthrough truth. A good catch from the nets I threw into the unconscious.

There is another picture saying "Honey is good with schizophrenic counselors." At the time of editing this in 2022--I will have another photo of Bokeh--"Bokeh is good with schizophrenic photogs."

There is a relationship between schizophrenia and photography.

In another sense my photographs seem to be boldly trying to overcome one tough situation or obstacle after another and to turn it to something beautiful and timely. Taking the dread disease of schizophrenia and finding tools to overcome obstacles and illness and then to open new doors or move mountains and overcome is where, not only photography, but any of the arts and writing comes in. One becomes a pioneer with this illness where others have dared to go or feared to go. Each photograph I do is seeming to be a choice towards responsibility and health and a choice to move towards beauty and freedom. While I will never be free of the dread disease of schizophrenia, my photography certainly gives me some freedoms and responsibility and creativity in becoming more stable and focused. In that sense, my remission from this illness has been longer and stronger. The work I do with photography and writing allows me to be more peaceful and have well-being. A good photograph is better than a drink or Puff the Magic Dragon or escaping reality with illness.

The Jungian disology (10 Jungian concepts with photographs) made with photographs representing the shadow, anima, animus, persona, self and conscious and unconscious was very healing. Photography seems to bring order out of chaos.

In some ways my photography and writing might give other people with the dread disease of schizophrenia or any of the other disorders out there--courage and permission to take risks and create or adventure where others have not gone as well.

December 28, 2019

At a point where the symptoms are in the form of victim thoughts for PTSD; a picture of that would be of something twisted or distorted perhaps.

Christmas came and went this week. It was a lovely Christmas—no hint of psychosis or thinking errors. Just well-being and good food and modest presents.

I slip into victim thinking the way someone would nurse a mixed drink—this is toxic and keeps me from snapping a picture.

January 10, 2020

Lowenthal's, et. al book is inspiring me to look more at a picture and look more at the "punctum" in the images I have selected here for this book on photography and schizophrenia. What is compelling emotionally in these pictures—that hurt, inspire, anger, or create joy can be associated with memories, grief, trauma and insight. In Lowenthal's book there was a Finnish woman who had the idea of pictures that have a non-verbal element to them and I was trying to read my facial expressions, moods and emotions in the pictures. What am I feeling? It's more than pictures to say "I AM." I think my self-portraits say: "I am schizophrenic, but I have value"; "I'm schizophrenic but I'm highly educated and trained, and I don't talk in word salads and I'm not psychotic—look—see here is a picture of me looking responsible and stable and creative."

High Brow Schizophrenia

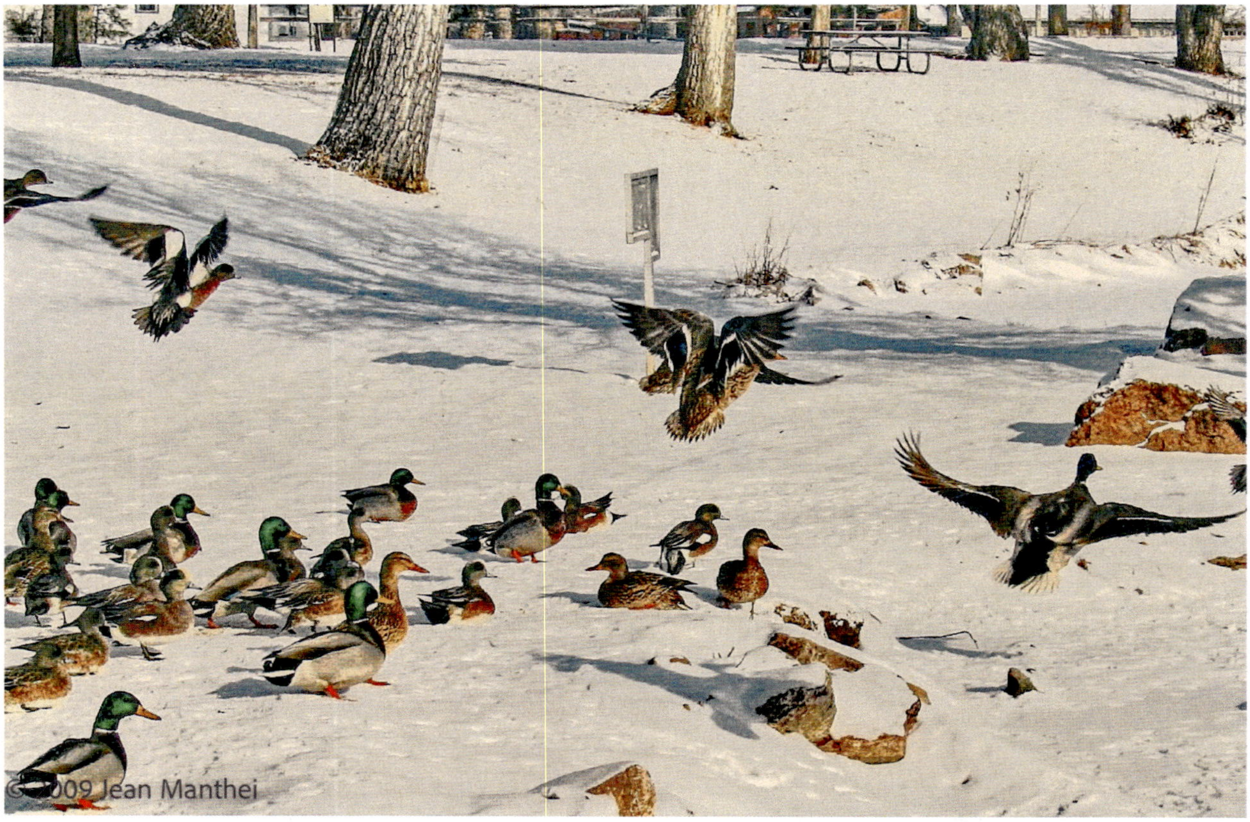
© 2009 Jean Manthei

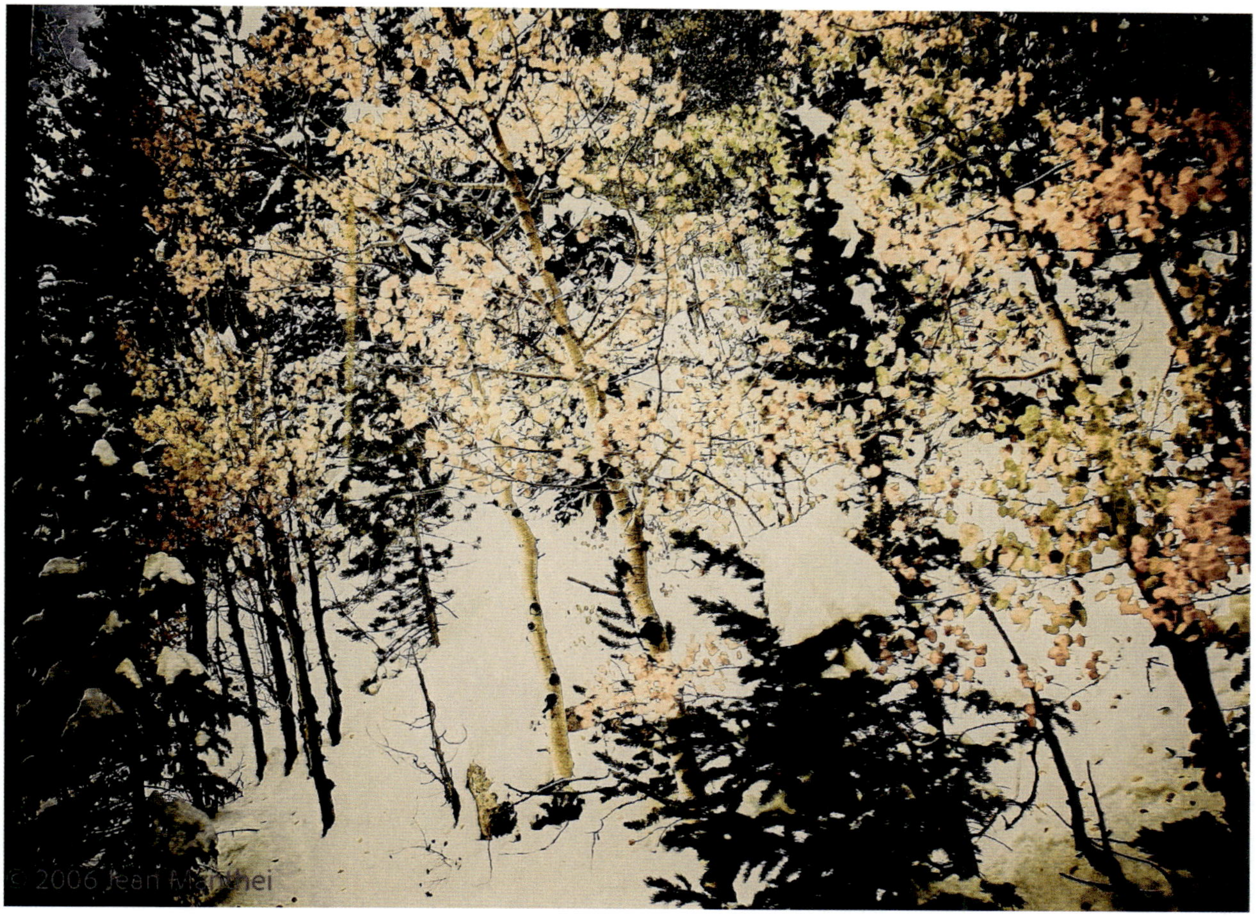
© 2006 Jean

This was in the Pieces of Mind Exhibit and was awarded to a state legislator in Colorado back in 2008. It was from the last time I saw my mom in 2007.

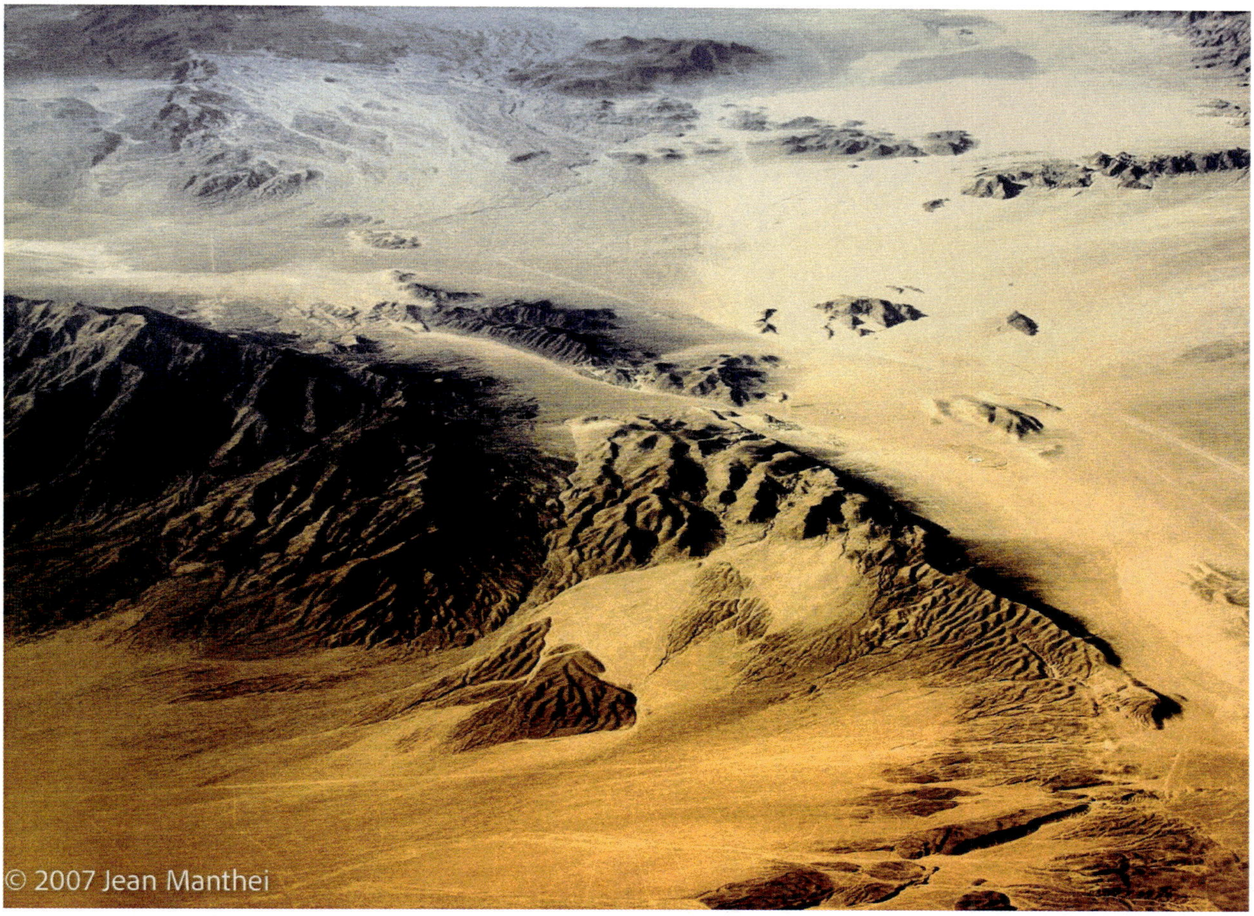
© 2007 Jean Manthei

© 2007 Jean Manthei

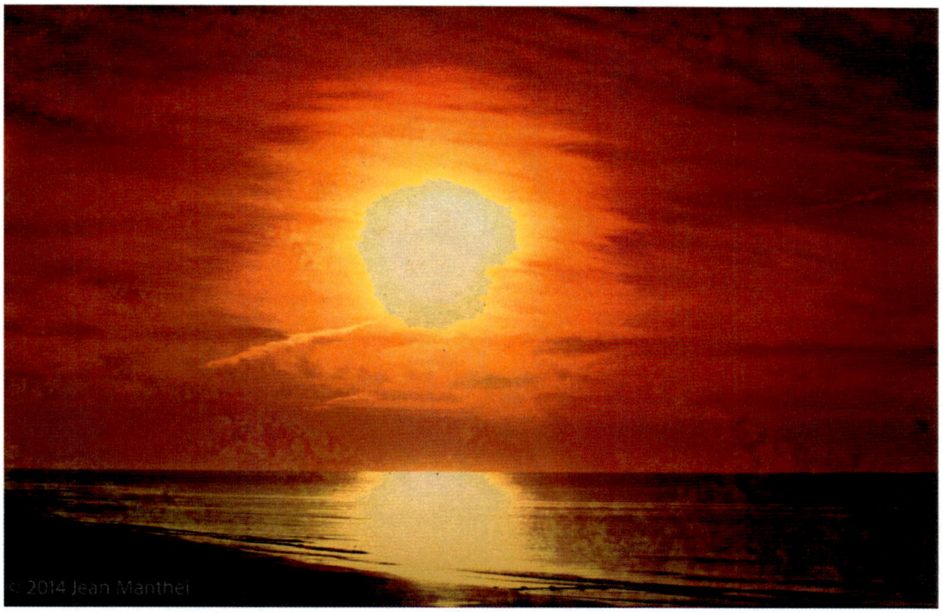
© 2014 Jean Manthei

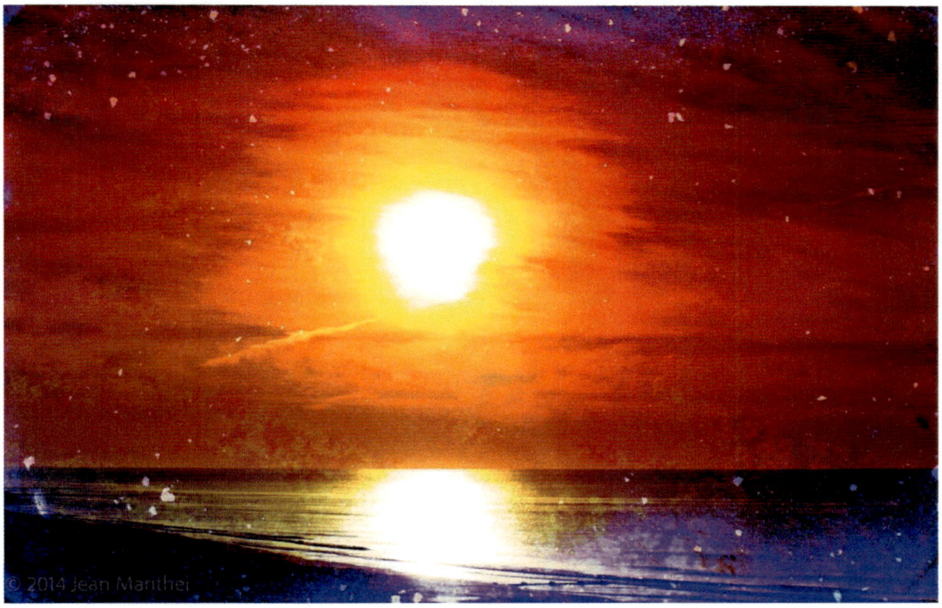
© 2014 Jean Manthei

© 2018 Jean Manthei

February 2, 2020

I've been on the hot seat in my six decades of treatment while people have exposed me and made attempts on my life. I would think they would be superstitious, and they'd become psychotic, hopeless, or clinically depressed for doing this to a schizophrenic all her life. I'd think their lives would become as unpleasant as they've made it for me. How do you convey that pain in a picture?

I tell you what I have instead is a picture of my hands clasped almost in prayer with my parents wedding bands on both hands. These were the rings of my parents for their 25th wedding anniversary. I sometimes feel they are joined now in love and to help me self-protect and protect me from harm's way and artful and designing people. There is peace when I fold my hands at night and think of them enveloping me with love and peace and the love that hath no understanding.

I really don't want to waste time on wishing any of the people that violated me or tried to kill me ill will because then I become unhealthy and that is not healthy or responsible. It's difficult because they haven't stopped and have me constantly in my amygdala. They hijack your mind.

At the AOD conference—Winter Symposium last week I learned about trauma and then I learned about trauma as it impacts the family systems and addictions and how things like food can greatly impact mood and well-being and bring peace. Went and bought a bunch of books like **Wheatbelly** and **Blue Kitchen Zones** and then went shopping today for things like Greek salad ingredients, gluten free tortillas, black beans and garbanzo beans and I'm getting Almond milk and I got nuts: cashews, pistachios, peanuts and romaine lettuce hearts. And Turmeric. As if all this would have me to live to 100 or somehow reduce my symptoms of schizophrenia, paranoia and anxiety, stress, and PTSD. It could.

It's not going to take away the PTSD the criminals caused. It's not going to undo 40 years of voices from the business. It's not going to take away pain from the crimes they committed against me. Have a handful of pistachios and a Greek salad. I did eat that tonight and I did feel contentment and well-being. Staying rooted in gratitude and naming the demons frees you.

Tomorrow I'll eat Greek salad again with a croissant and gluten free tortilla with beans, sour cream and avocado and some yogurt and I'll take a picture of it to capture well-being.

February 16, 2020

My dad would be 106 tomorrow. I celebrated Valentine's Day this year. A good time to take stock in one's relationships. I don't have a meaningful relationship with a significant other. And I'm not sure with this illness that it is fair to a spouse or kids to subject them to your illness. My relationships with people are honest and from the heart.

Tonight, I am hating my schizophrenia—it is mixed with agitation, anxiety, depression and fear and anger and victim thinking. Plus, I've had my fair share of thinking errors and PTSD thoughts lately. When I'm feeling good, and my perceptions are not distorted and I'm playful and creative this illness is manageable. Sometimes interesting and humorous and fun. I don't want you to get the wrong idea of this illness—some days like this last week were hell. And there was hopelessness and the fears that society would perish.

When I'm lost and hopeless, I'm not feeling like picking up a camera. I had planned on taking pictures of the purple calla lilies, but they came for Valentine's Day, and some had frozen with leaves that looked like cooked spinach and there were broken lilies. I wanted to take some pictures of something hopeful. That's about the only thing I would have had energy to take a picture of and it would certainly not reflect this doom and gloom. I don't know that I would want to take a picture of this depressing bunch of feelings.

I had thought things this week that people had misused their power and energies and that when society does that, they lose energy and power when they hurt people and destroy lives. How do you take a picture of that and how it left you feeling? I can't think in terms of metaphor tonight; yet, my book, ***Recovery Book for Clinicians***, is filled with idioms and photographs that I made when I was healthier and feeling better. I can't think for the life of me of a metaphor for the pain I was experiencing.

I have had this curious Fitbit, Versa 2 watch that can upload my pictures to and I'm very happy about that. I bought this watch, and it came in a special box for Valentine's Day to put the assortment of Versa 2 watchbands in. I can set an alarm to get up. I can do breath relaxations and then with this premium thing I can get apps that talk you through mindfulness exercises to reduce anxiety and stress.

February 23, 2020

I went to see a Mozart concert last night.
The next four pictures were taken around February 17, 2020. That was my dad's 106th birthday. Worked with the photographs in Luminar 4.

I was thinking after roughly 6 decades of treatment and all this education there should have been some happier endings here. No one should be in this kind of pain and difficulty in society after decades of treatment like this. I pay taxes, I work and serve the community; I do the right things, I've done my psychiatric time not to be dangerous to self or others, keep up my household, I play nice with others. I work hard in my own treatment. I shouldn't be fearing that people were going to end my life. I shouldn't feel violated and shouldn't be in harm's way. I shouldn't feel like people are trying to take my identity and intellectual property.

February 24, 2020

Today wasn't a whole lot better. I did manage to work on the computer. I worked on the Windows partition of the computer. Worked on the DavidJournal which gives journal prompts for spiritual or ideas for journal entries and there is one for creative writing. Changed the desktop slideshow and the home screen picture. Entered dreams. Have this dream project I've been working on—I have a journal filled with dreams from the 1980s and 1990s and I've been typing up 3 or 4 dreams a day and entering that into the Alchera software program which has a dictionary of symbols and you can add your own symbols and definitions and then give general impressions, current concerns and conclusions. It's pretty good and as I've gone along, I've honed skills at dream interpretation, putting together conclusions and ideas I might not have seen back then. I've asked for some dreams that would be able to put into perspective some of what those dreams might have meant or taught me in going back and working with them. In the ***Dreamer's United*** version of the Alchera software you can add photographs and I've tried to insert photos that captured the essence of more recent dreams.

March 13, 2020

A blizzard. For about three weeks prior to last week, I stressed whether my sister-in-law went to the dark side and violated the trust because she, it later turned out, forgot to deposit my stipend and was out of the country. Then I thought my birth daughter decided maybe she didn't like me because I hadn't heard from her in 3 months. But she said she was sick for a month and then they travelled. My computer malfunctioned and I had to call Geek Squad to come fix it. When they got here, they fixed it in 5 minutes. It could have been a lot worse if he hadn't been able to put in a code to restore its function—sometimes he said you must get a whole new computer. I was able
to use my work check to cover automatic withdrawals for health and car

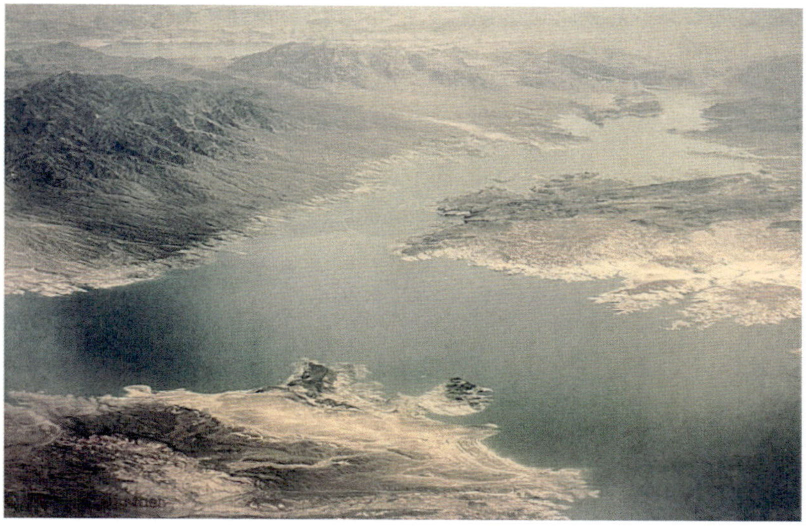

2019. One of the assignments in ***Zen Camera*** by David Ulrich was to take some pictures to find your essence using windows and mirrors and objects.

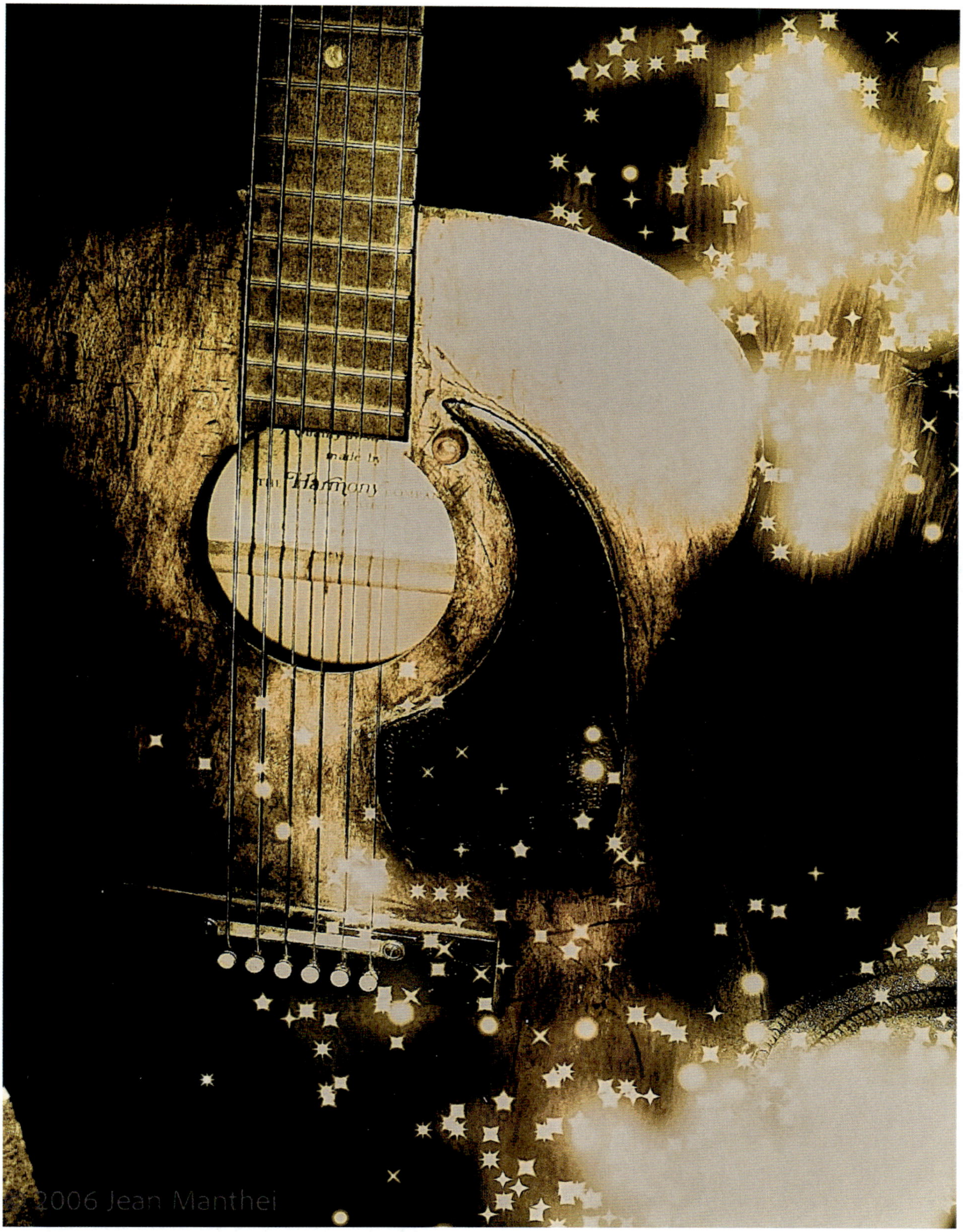
made in
Harmony
2006 Jean Manthei

The pictures I got of the Claremont train station are used by permission from the Los Angeles Metrolink.

insurance and Creative Cloud and things. I went to therapy and didn't stew too much after I practiced some skills in letting go. Ten days later I heard from my sister-in-law. Sometimes time itself resolves problems as it did in this case, but not always.

I did another piece on overspending and grief. I was looking to work with PTSD, schizophrenia, fear, grief, being in harm's way as the things that needed to be addressed underlying a lot of overspending. The thought was that the spending might be resolved with fiscal responsibility if I took care of some of these other issues. The presenting issue is fiscal responsibility—the real issue is being in harm's way. Sometimes the real problems can't be addressed. The idea that if you address the real problems of underlying symptoms, problem behaviors can then be overcome was the idea put forth by Claudia Black in ***Changing Course*** in working with underlying grief (Black, 2002). It was the idea of addressing real issues before problems can be solved has become common knowledge in the field of psychology and addictions, i.e., family systems theory proposed by Watzlawick, Bateson, and Haley in the 1960s. But in Ms. Black's book it suddenly turned on a light or two and I heard that at much deeper levels.

Have noticed a change in my compulsions to overspend when I worked on the project to overcome spending and address the real issues. And then came the Yeti tumblers and mugs. I used my debit card for those. Have not done mindless shopping in maybe a week since working on my money project.

How would you take a picture of fiscal responsibility when you have schizophrenia?

This month shopped for Covid19 in case we get quarantined. I have enough soup to last a month. The pandemic diet. The pandemic quickly put into perspective what is and is not important in life and has sort of taken the wind out of the sails of spending.

I don't think in my time alive there has been anything like this kind of worldwide pandemic. I'm much less in denial this week as they closed

2020 Jean Manthei

OMG!
Ketu is good with
schizophrenic authors
JOKER
JOKER
© 2016 Jean Manthei

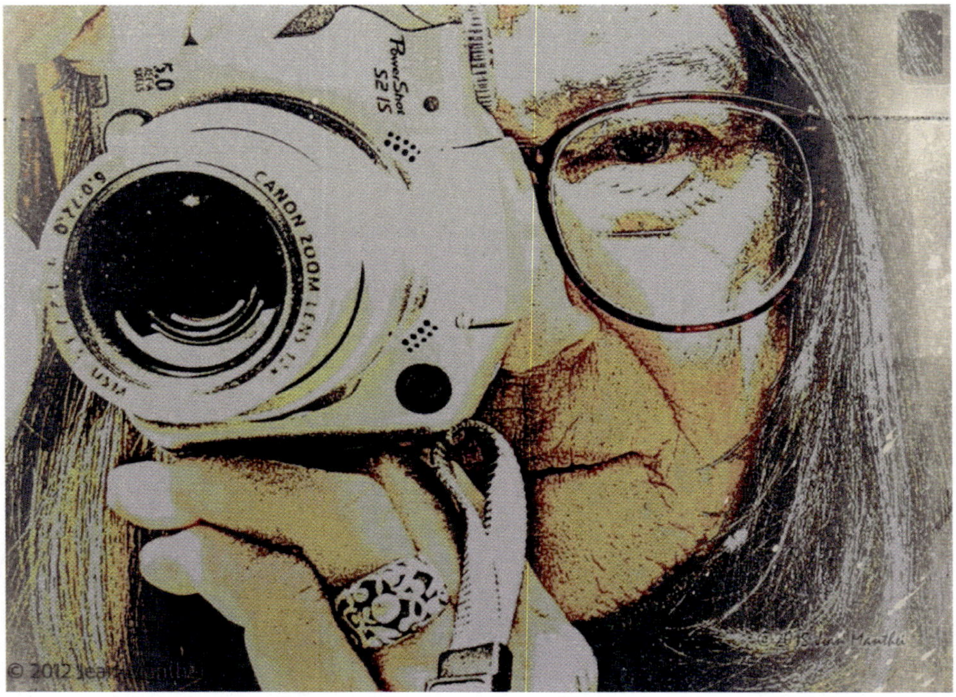
PowerShot
S2 IS
CANON ZOOM LENS

Picture taken in 2020 on my 70th birthday by Chris Haynes. In post-production I added the effects. This was in year two of Covid19.

my church until the end of the month and likewise the NicA meetings I hold there. Work is still open. Wonder if they will cancel the Philharmonic concerts this year. [They did and the church was closed a couple of years—4-24-22]

There was something special about the Yeti tumblers.

I got 4 books bound last weekend that contain dreams I was working on entering from the 1980s and 1990s. They will be interesting to sit down and read some time. There must be 800-1000 pages. A lot of that is repetition of dream dictionary words and dreams that were already entered that connect to the dream worked on. Maybe 100 pages in the four books are dreams.

The only photography in the last month and a half has been the calla lilies and the moon. I used the macro lens on some of the calla lilies.

When I've been anxious or fears that creep in about neighbors and community I am not motivated to take pictures. I'm not likely to go down that neuropathway and I must force myself instead to pick up my camera.

Sometimes those non-verbal cues and abuse lead me to wonder about other people who have hurt me—whatever happened to those folks—did they live happily ever after with no consequences; did anyone ever take them or their children off the deep end and try to kill them? Did any of those people suffer any of the misfortunes that they caused me? Did any of their children become disabled with people like themselves harming their kids? My higher self descended at that point and put a stop to that line of thinking "you can do Photoshop, Luminar, Lightroom, you can apply presets, paint in clouds and you can go and snap pictures—you may not fantasize or delight in the misfortune of others even if they have done you grave harm and injustice." And that jolted me right out of negativity and anger and into humanity and

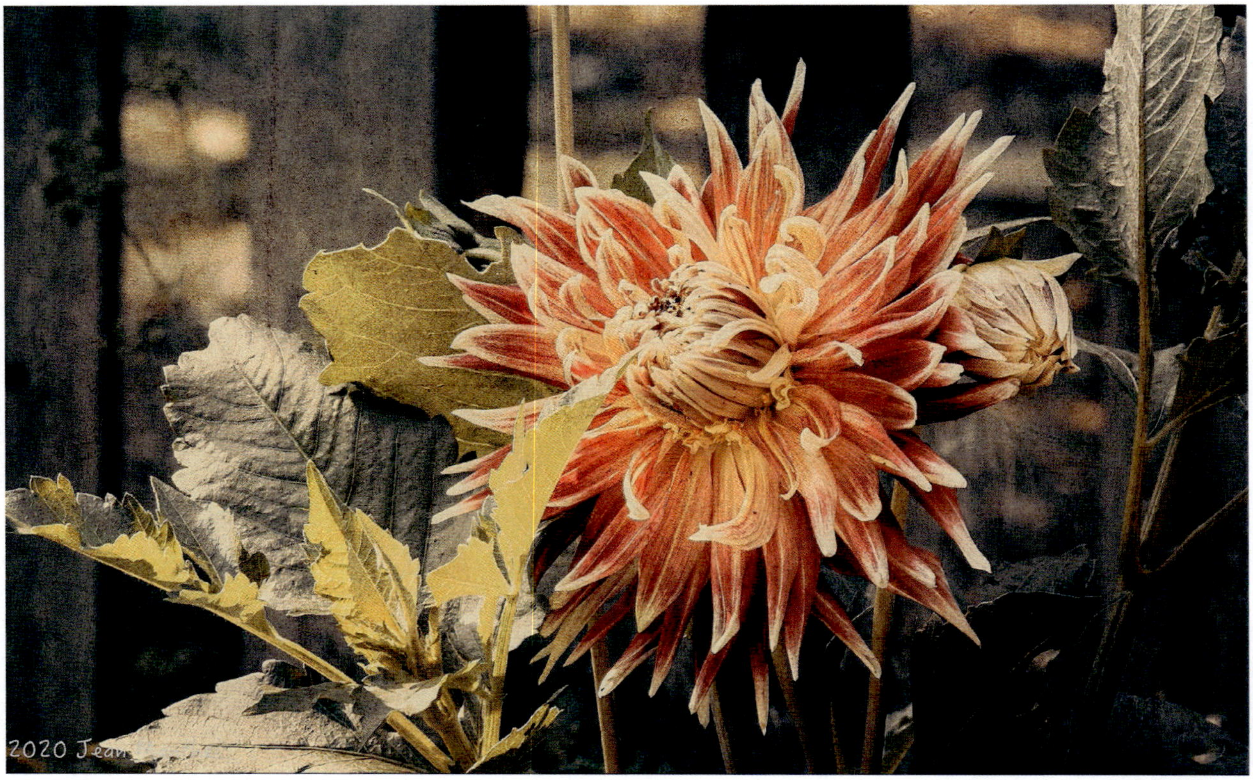
2020 Jean

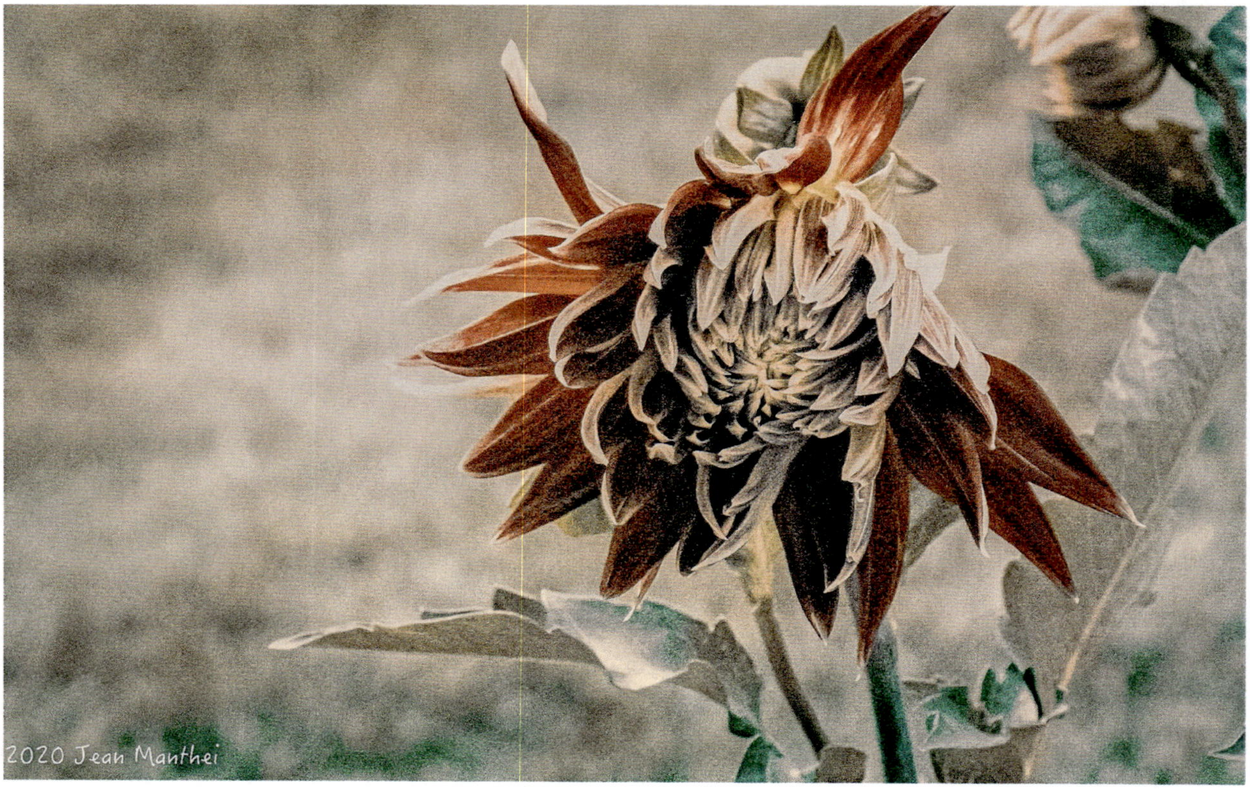
2020 Jean Manthei

No time to be schizophrenic if you are snapping pictures

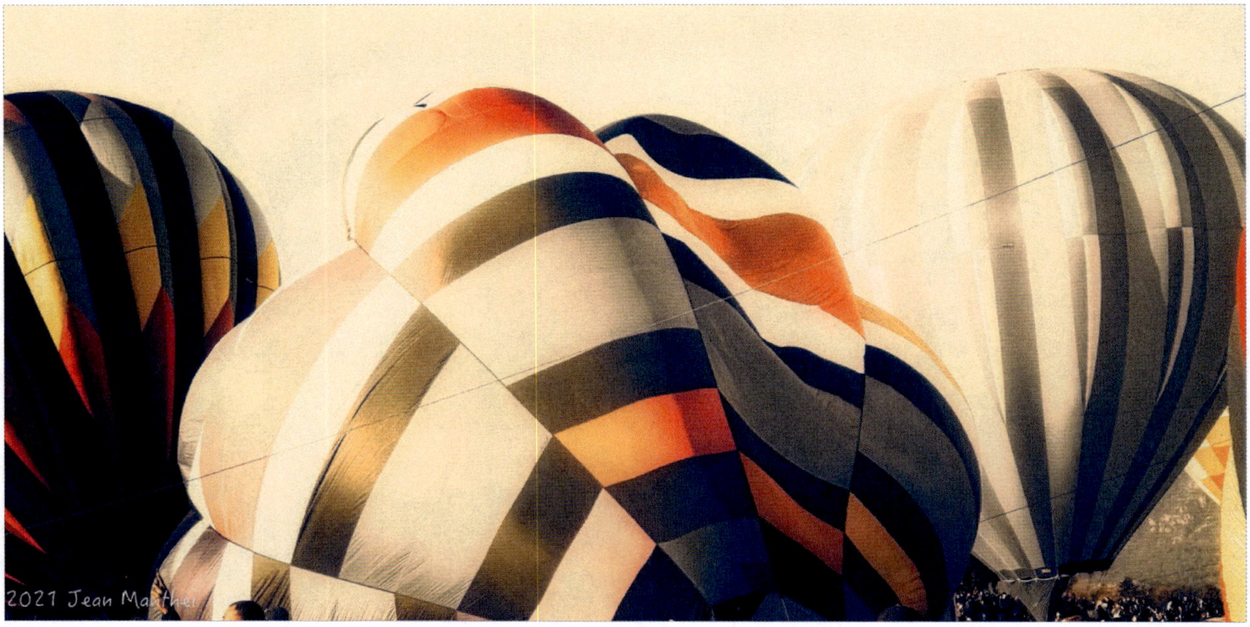
2021 Jean Manthei

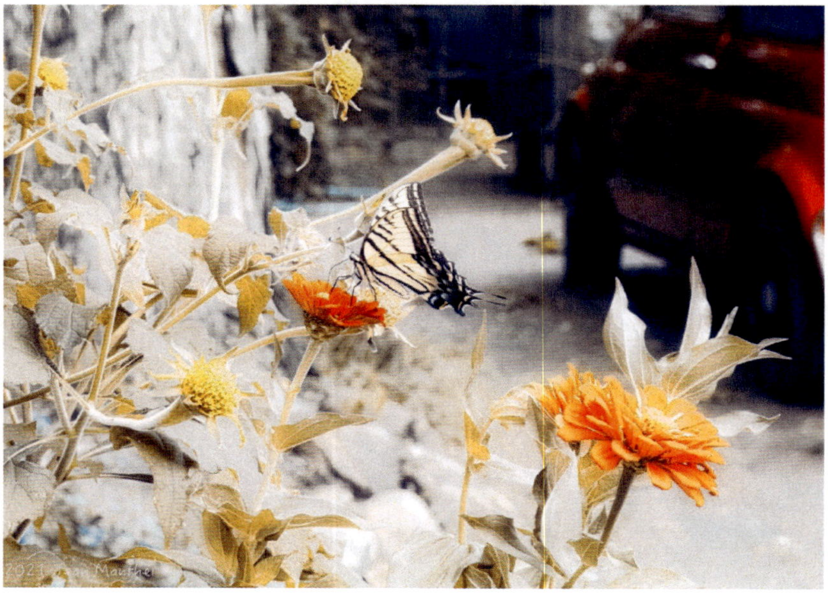

© 2019 Jean Manthei

creativity where my spiritual center and God would have me focus my energy.

March 22, 2020
The pandemic is sweeping the country. Covid19. And there's even the tobacco racketeers trying to make me relapse and decompensate to smoking and psychosis in the middle of this pandemic. Low brow. The tricky dicks that made me suicidal for 2 years where I didn't want to live (back in 1979 to 1981 and 1973 to 1975) haven't ever had to be the victims of their abuse and murder attempts. Added cheer to the pandemic. What to snap a picture of. The calla lilies. The local news was reporting that people were using Everclear for hand sanitizer and hording beer like people were hording toilet paper.

If I pass away from Covid19 I won't be able to finish this book. I won't be able to continue to overcome this dread disease of schizophrenia.

April 10, 2020
A Covid19 isolation picture. [My drone picture that I placed in an Adobe stock image]. I still work because I'm considered essential personnel. Other than that, I don't leave my house. We're doing tele-therapy at work. It is surreal doing a group in an empty room on an iPad. I prayed I wouldn't decompensate in this pandemic. Was more worried about that then getting Covid 19.

I guess I've come to the end of what I can say about photography and schizophrenia. My hope is that this is something that will inspire you or give you more hope—particularly if you have this dread disease of schizophrenia. And that you'll get an appreciation of the use of photography when you have this or any of the other disorders in the *DSM-V*. It's another connection to the soul and to healing, health, dreams, and creativity in the reduction of symptoms-at least of schizophrenia. Maybe diagnosis shouldn't matter if you have a feel and eye for photography.

And in doing all that it deepens one's thoughts and depth in being more appreciative of the role of meaning and purpose in life and art. It gives a person something else to do and think about besides the dread disease of schizophrenia and in so doing there is less time left over to be schizophrenic and more time to focus on something imaginative and creative. If you were alcoholic and you were into photography as part of your recovery maybe there would be less time to think about drinking or drugs. If you were antisocial and hostile or aggressive and unfriendly there would be less time for hurting others and doing bodily harm and acting out if you were into the real estate of photography.

In having less time for schizophrenia because I have a camera or a journal in my hand—I can pretend for some brief moments that I'm a photog great, an artist and I can also return refreshed to my work as a counselor who also happens to have schizophrenia.

In 2023 I will have had sixty years of treatment, and this has helped me build a psychological and emotional house that isn't haunted, but is stable and that has interesting nooks and crannies, novelty—a home with a top floor and an attic and mid-floor and ground level and basement. It's a hospitable home to enter with a playful inner child whose name is Igloo (who has inspired me to be responsible despite schizophrenia). And in my home, there are lots of play things and things that weren't in this house or personality when I moved in here in 1983. A book I published sits on one of the shelves and lots of journals about the continuing saga of schizophrenia. There's a conscious and unconscious. The house (me) has character and personality and lots of "look what I made in therapy" of 16x20 metal prints on all the walls that depict things I've worked hard on and for and from which some important healing took place in the decades of treatment that I've been to. And all that work shows and has paid off.

There is no way you could take a picture of the experience of being on the hotseat of therapy since 1963. What's a good photograph of psychiatric assault? It's like being in a fishbowl with unauthorized people stealing your personality

parts and thoughts and feelings from you and your counselor because they can get access to your life, treatment and relationships, college campuses and personal experiences. My therapist sure doesn't expose me. It's like the Fielding-Elsberg psychiatric break-in. You could snap a pretty good picture of that with symbols. What I want to be focused on is a different way to use light and consciousness and awareness and my camera.
The end.

Epilogue

BOKEH

This is going into the 3rd year of Covid 19. Honey, the dog I inherited from my brother Peter when he passed away, died in September of 2021. In December 2021 Bokeh came into my life with Honey and Ketu and Solo and Brie's spirits helping me find her. Bokeh are the effects in photographs of the roundish lights in the back of photographs. Bokeh became the light in the darkness of this pandemic and the loss of my family over the years. Bokeh is helping heal the wounds and trauma and illness.

There is so much pain in life and people are suffering. People weren't meant to suffer like this. I create in the face of adversity and illness and pain. There is no other alternative.

Since I completed *Photography and Schizophrenia* in 2019 or 2020 my photography has taken off in terms of quality and character. In the fall of 2021, I noticed a difference. It was with the pictures I later entered here of the Balloon Classic, fall on Prospect Street and the Akita dahlias and butterflies (Corelli and Bach that year) and Bokeh that was now capturing remission to my illness as well as a blossoming capacity to love again with the Golden Retriever for the golden birthday of smobriety. My work started coming into its own character and style. Maybe more than anything of expressing anything illness related, it was expressing myself as a photographer in a way that helped my self-worth and value for my talent as a human being independent of any role such as schizophrenic, photographer or LPC, CAS. The work I was doing had an-other worldly spiritual element to it in terms of getting down to the nitty gritty in life and the nature of life and death existential issues.

Instead of it being so much about illness--it was a search for meaning and purpose in the face of the pandemic and difficulties facing our society with violence and acting out, recovery issues and feeling as if I was in harm's way. I guess that if it's just schizophrenia or depression I wasn't fearful of losing my life--I figured I would be around to go to treatment or work. I didn't live in fear of the pandemic or some hitman. You are under the illusion that you will have time behind the lens to explore your sad little life--but that you will be alive to do so. You feel like you will be around to work with tough issues and tough perceptions with the camera or the pen. My book of photography and schizophrenia became more photography and life and death with the dread disease of schizophrenia. It kind of sobers you up out of symptoms and depression and thinking errors to tend to your life and to stay alive--the hope is for peace and that there might be time to explore the annals of photography and schizophrenia once again. If you have not met safety issues as outlined in Maslow's Hierarchy of Needs it is hard to self-actualize. I do self-actualize, in spite of issues, and I am grateful I am not psychotic to where I wouldn't feel like snapping a picture let alone writing. I feel grateful to be in remission this long. I can still focus. The pandemic brought a screeching halt to my fears around my illness.

Tragedy, life and death concerns, and illness snap you right out of your illness--because you in fact want to be alive to work with symptoms should they arise, and you can't do that if they kill you or make you suicidal and the pandemic overtakes you. One day and one thing at a time.

© 2022 Jean Manthei

Remission from Schizophrenia. Celebrating the joys and hardships of schizophrenia and overcoming substantial loss to become a very real human being. The illness doesn't go away--you just manage better.

2022 Jean Manthei

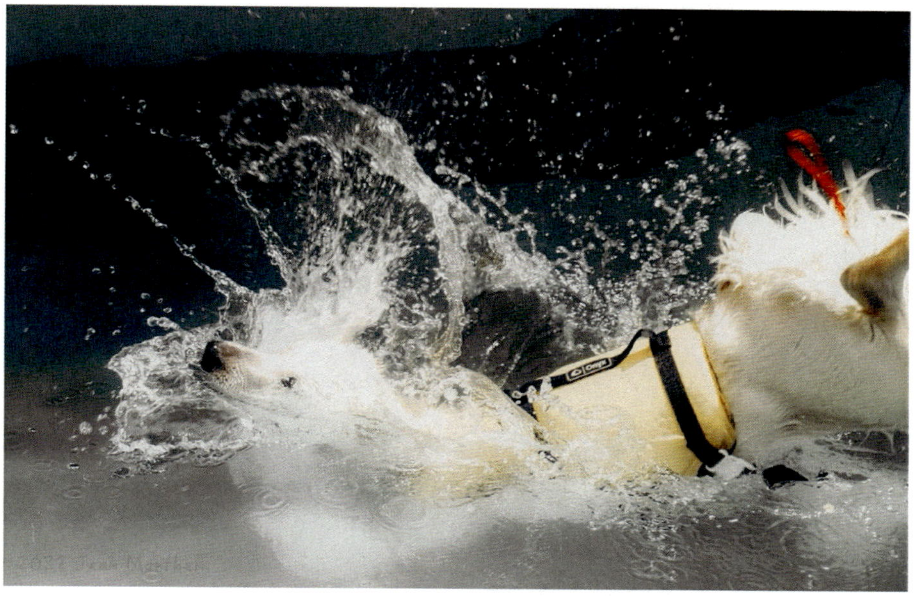

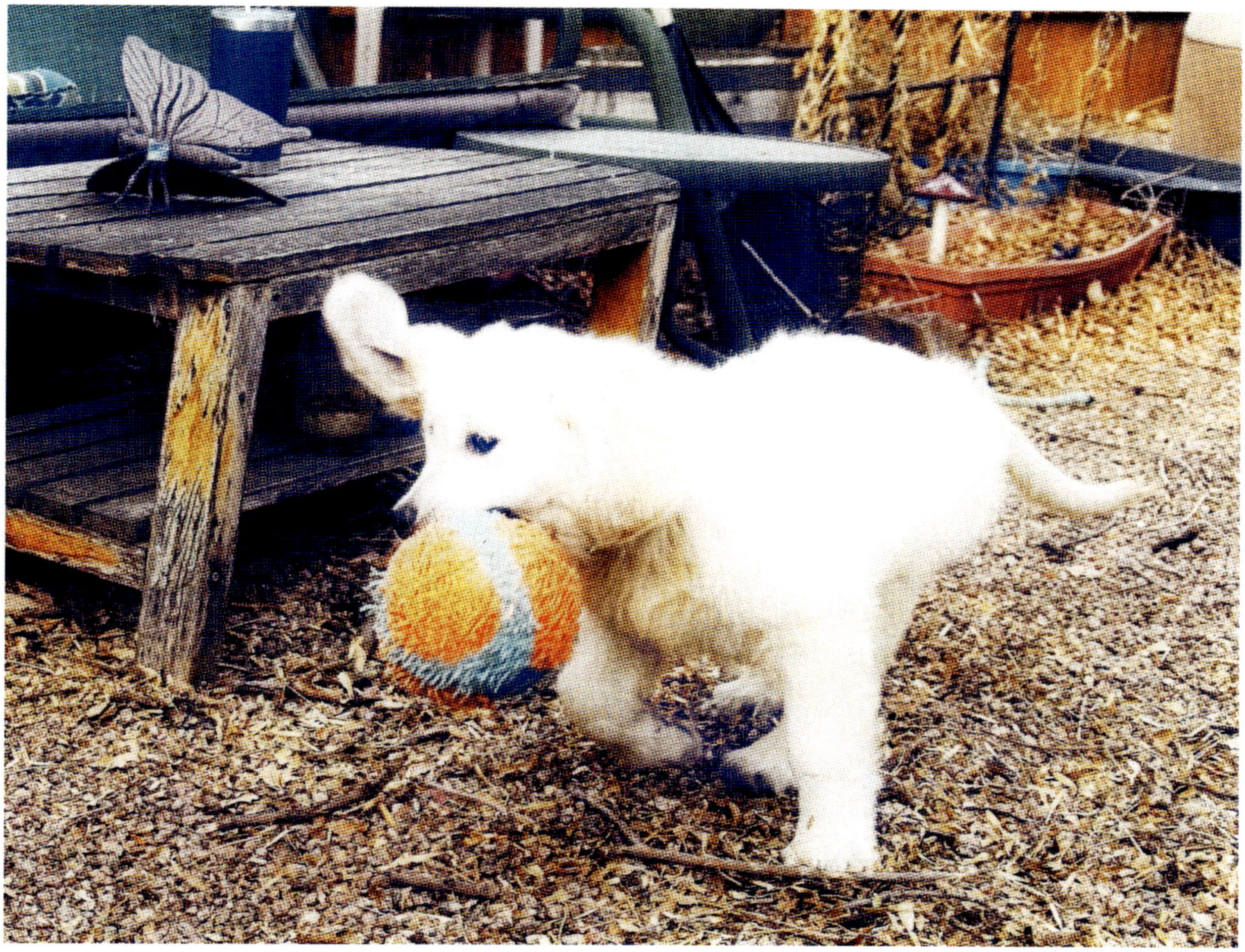

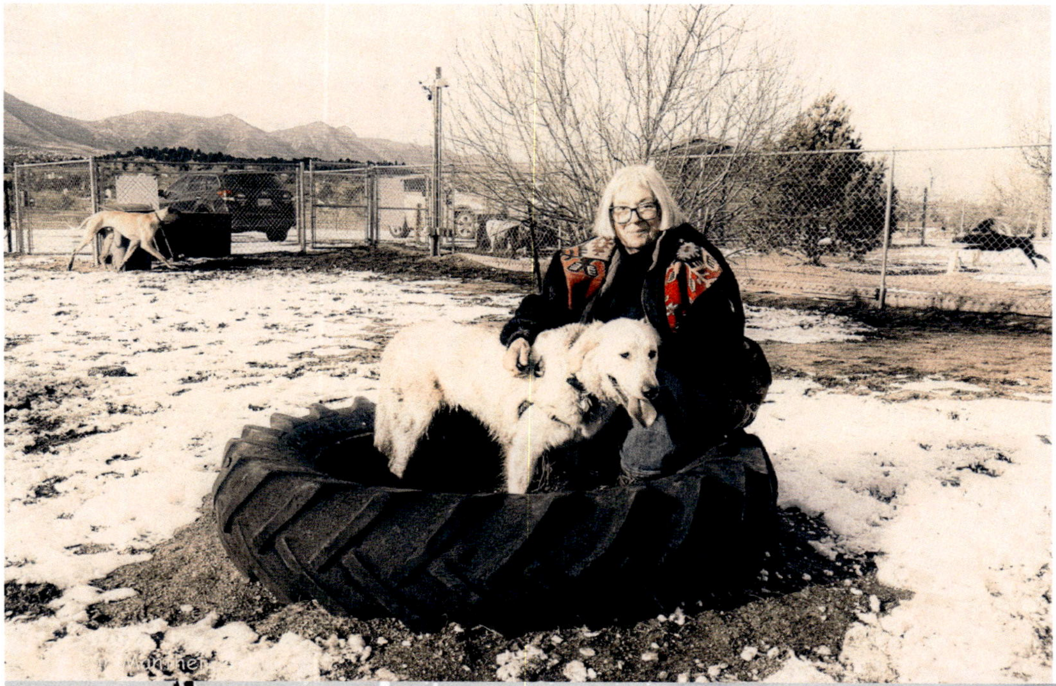

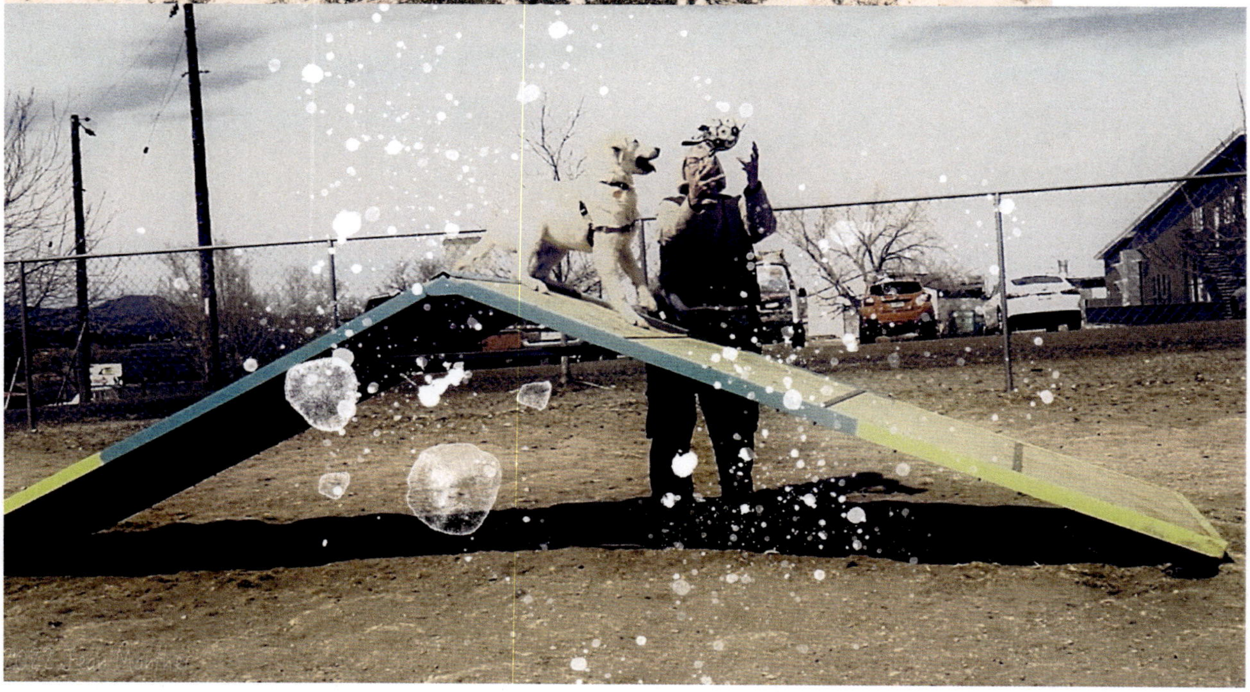

© 2023 Jean Manthei

Bokeh as a puppy—soon after I brought her home in December 2021.

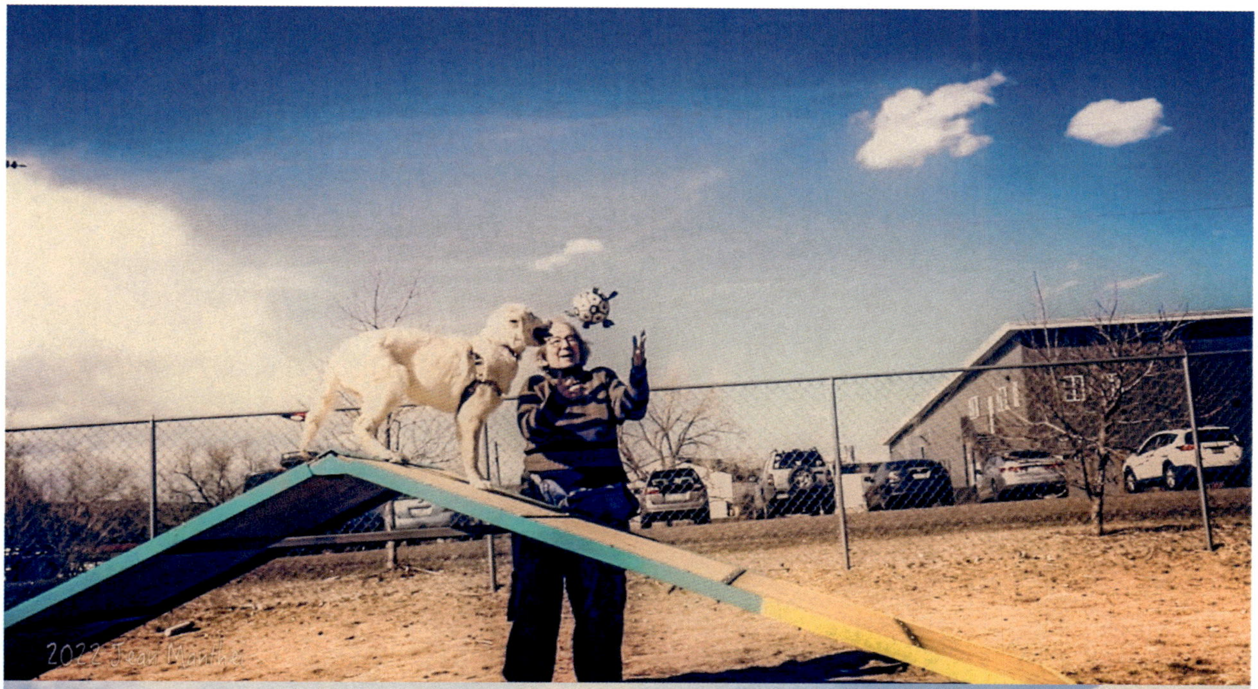
2022 Jean

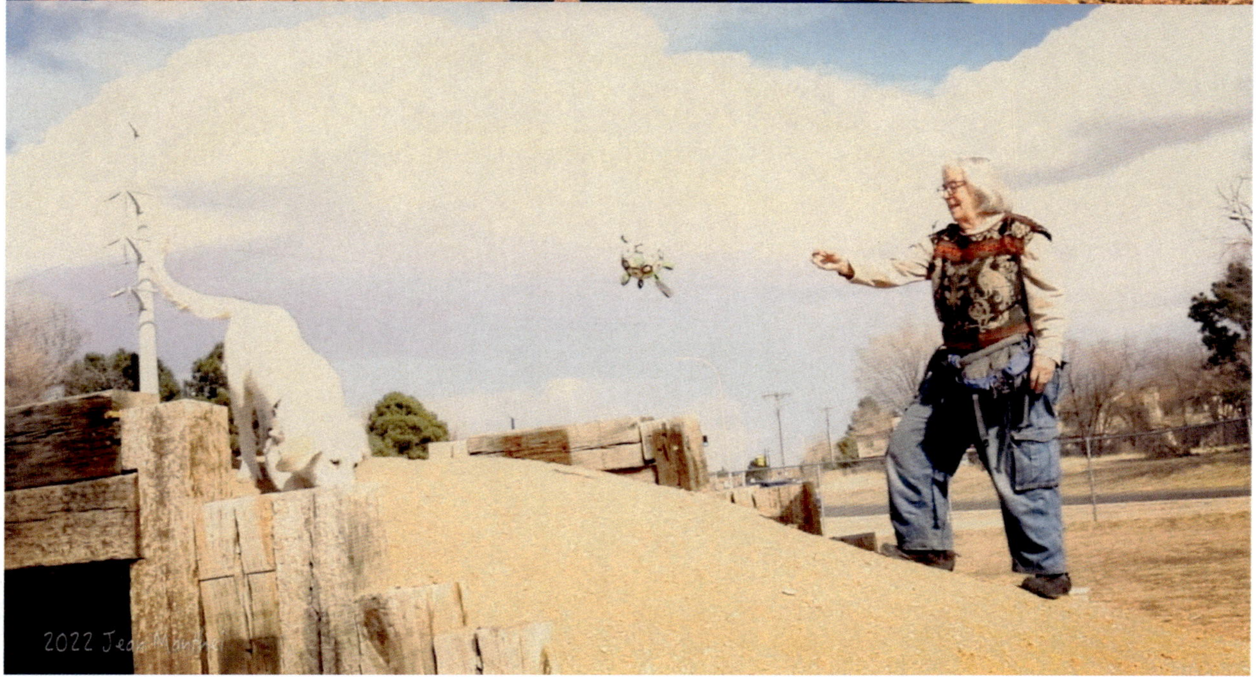
2022 Jean

I wanted her to be a therapy dog—but Bokeh is therapeutic, but I'm not sure she will ever be a therapy dog.

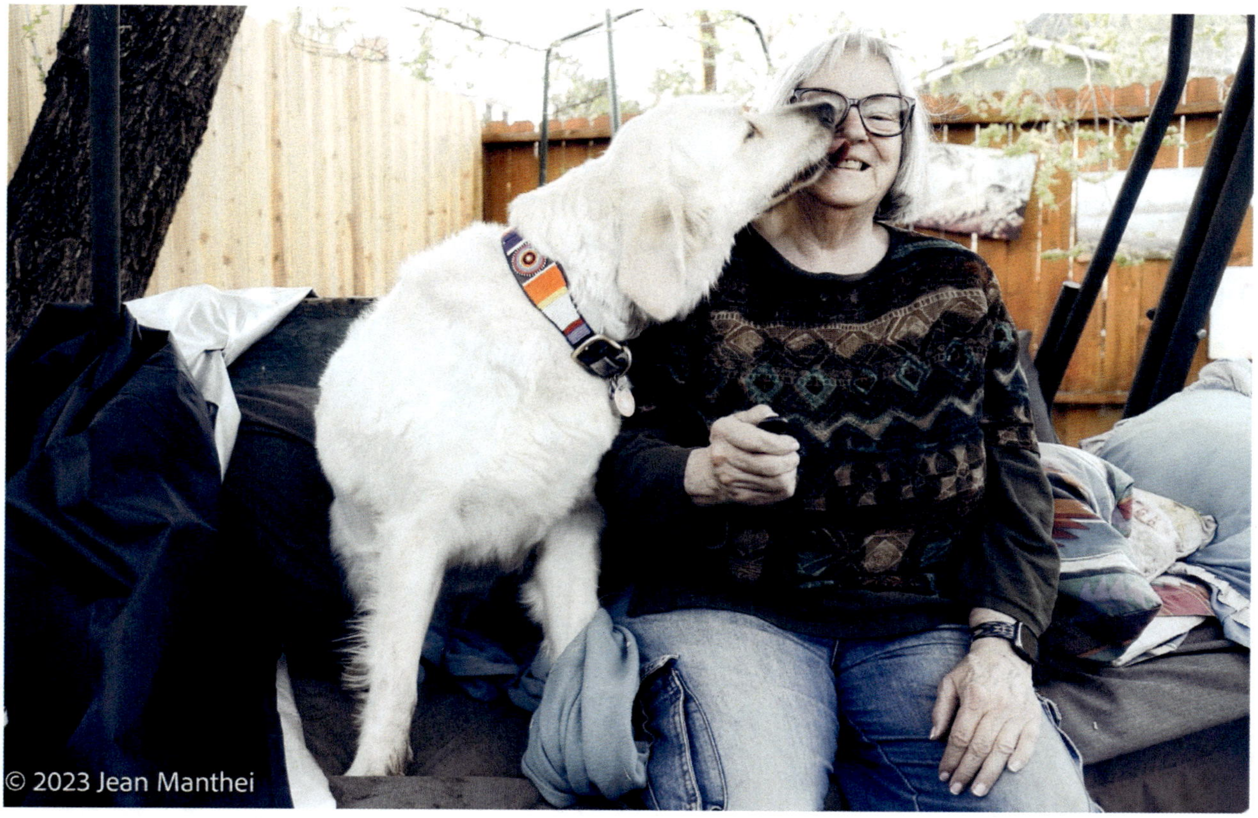

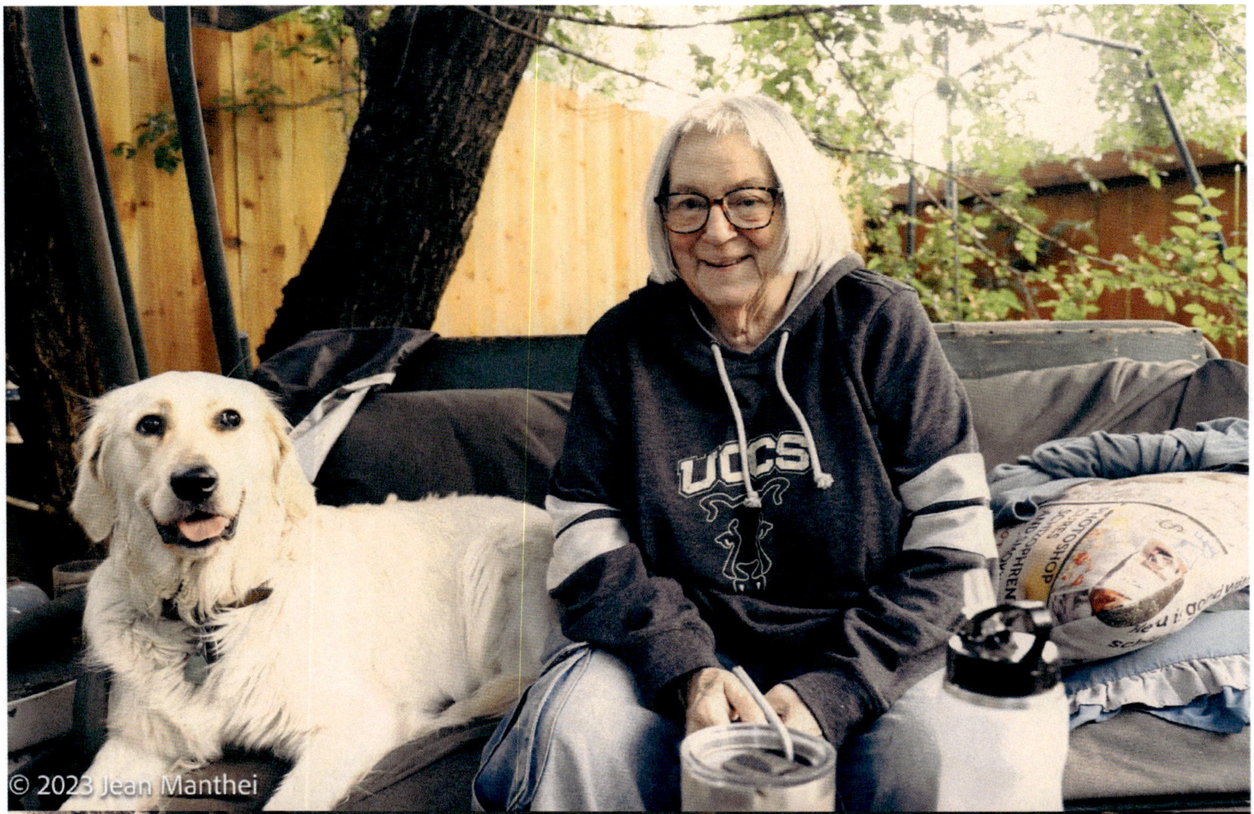
UCCS
© 2023 Jean Manthei

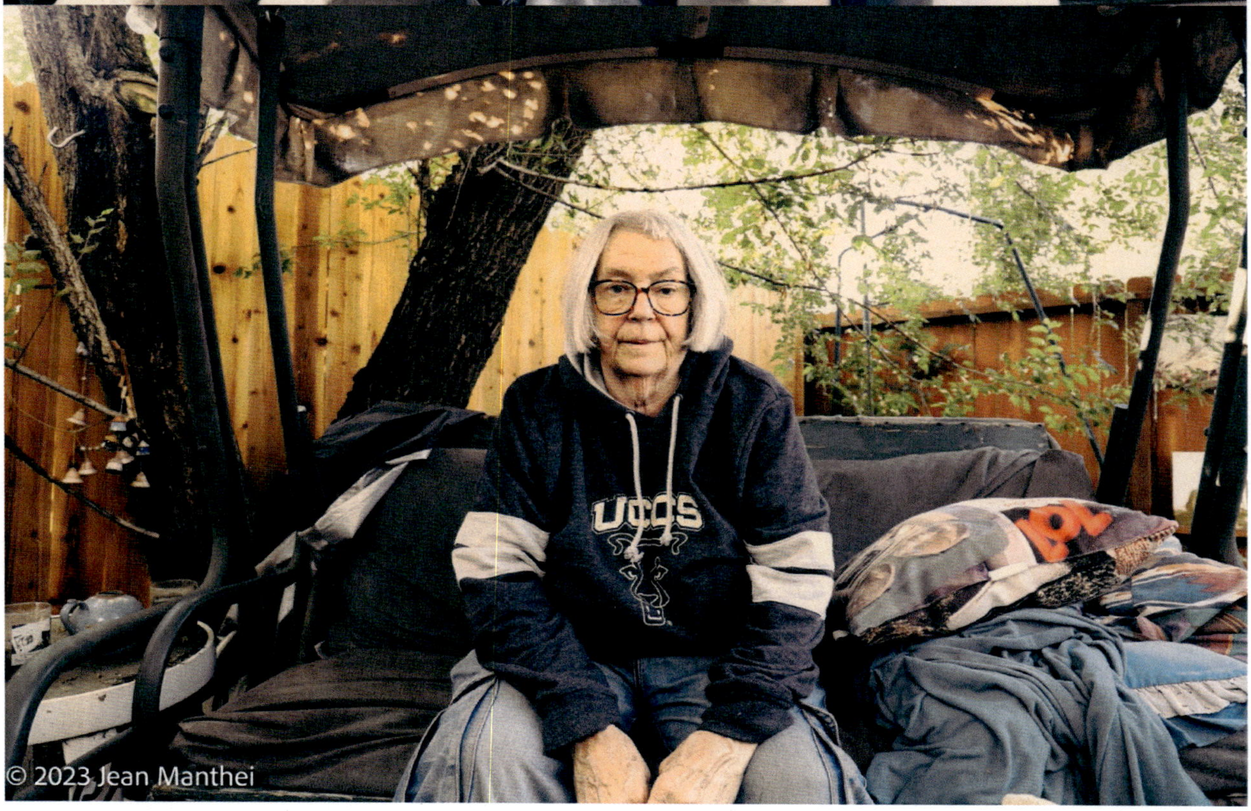
UCCS
© 2023 Jean Manthei

© 2023 Jean Manthei

A new book from UCCS Alum Jean Manthei

PHOTOGRAPHY AND SCHIZOPHRENIA

Hardcover $25 | Paperback $20

Jean Manthei, MA, LPC, CACIII
Alumni of UCCS (1992), Counselor and Author

Photography and Schizophrenia is a schizophrenic therapist's work with photography and her illess with important images she has captured that express hope and beauty instead of fragmentation and despair.

Jean-Marie Manthei graduated from UCCS with a Master's Degree in Counseling and Human Services. She has been a counselor in the field of addictions since 1993, and uses photography, writing and video work to describe what it is to live with a disability and work as a professional.

UCCS Bookstore

© 2023 Jean Manthei

© 2023 Teri Ulrich

2022 Jean Manthei

Bibliography

Bessel van der Kolk, M. (2014). *The Body Keeps the Score. Brain, Mind, and Body in the Healing of Trauma.* New York, New York: Penguin Books.

Black, Claudia Ph.D. (2002). *Changing Course*, 2nd ed. Center City, MN: Hazelden.

Bray, S. (2014). *Photography and Zen.* Discovering Your True Nature Through Photography. Internet: photographyandconsciousness.com.

Bray, S. (2015). *Photography and Psychoanalysis.* The Development of Emotional Persuasion in Image Making. Internet: photography and consciousness.com.

Craig, C. (2009). *Exploring the Self Through Photography.* Activities For use in group work. London, UK: Jessica Kingsley Publishers.

Devries, D. (2019). *Contemplative Vision Photography as a Spiritual Practice.* New York, NY: Church Publishing Incorporated.

Fryrear, J.L. (1992). *Photo Art Therapy: A Jungian Perspective.* Springfield, IL: Charles C Thomas Publishers.

Gibson, N. (2018. *Therapeutic Photography. Enhancing Self-esteem, Self-efficacy and Resilience.* London, UK: Jessica Kingsley Publishers.

Hood, D.A. (2019). *Shutter Therapy Photography and Muse for the Soul.* Coppell, TX: Internet: statusimage.com

Isenhower, V.K. (2012). *Meditation on Both Sides of the Camera: A Spiritual Journey in Photography.* Nashville, TN: Upper Room Books.

Kelby, S. (2007). *The Digital Photography Book.* San Francisco, CA: Peachpit Press.

Kubie, L.L. M.D. (1961). *The Neurotic Distortion of the Creative Process.* New York, NY: The Noonday Press.

Loewenthal, D. E. (2013). *Phototherapy and Therapeutic Photography in the Digital Age.* Hove, Sussex, Routledge

Manthei, J. M. MA, LPC, CAS (2010). *On Gratitude.* Durham, CT: Eloquent Books.

Menninger, K. (1963). *The Vital Balance.* New York, NY: The Viking Press.

Painter, C.V. (2013). *Eyes of the Heart Photography.* Notre Dame, IN: Sori Books.

Phillips J. (2000). *God is at Eye Level: Photography as a Healing Art.* Wheaton, IL: Quest Books: Theosophical Publishing House.

Sammon, R. (2019). *Photo Therapy: Motivation and Wisdom. Discovering the Power of Pictures.* Independently published.

Shapiro, P.L. (2001). *The Tao of Photography.* New York, NY: Ten Speed press, Division of Random House.

Shusterman, N. (2015). *Challenger Deep.* New York, NY: Harper Teen Harper Collins.

Ulrich, D. (2018). *Zen Camera.* New York, NY: Watson-Guptill Publications.

Ulrich, D. (2002). *The Widening Stream.* Hillsboro, OR: Beyond Words Publishing.

Weiser, J.P. Ph.D. (1993). *Phototherapy Techniques.* San Francisco, CA: Jossey-Bass Publishers.

Wong, D.K. (2015). *How Photography Helped in Self-Healing.* Internet: Publisher: Smashwords, Inc.

Wood, A.K. (2011). *The Practice of Contemplative Photography: Seeing the World with Fresh Eyes.* Boston, MA: Shambhala.

Zehr, H. (2005). *The Little Book of Contemplative Photography.* Intercourse, PA: Good Books.

Index

Blue Moon 126, 127, 128

Diagnosis shouldn't matter 139, 175

Exercises for Readers 60-61

   Schizophrenia 61
   Antisocial 61, 175
   Borderline 62
   Major Clinical Depression 62
   PTSD 135, 154

Ghosts and spirits 12, 40

Carl Jung 20, 143

Life & Death/snapping you out of illness briefly 179-180

Other authors mentioned

  Stephen Bray 109
  V.K. Isenhower 109
  Scott Kelby 22
  Lawrence Kubie 50
  Lowenthal 144
  Judy Weiser 18
  Karl Menninger 60
  Jan Phillips 109
  David Ulrich 109

Overspending, life and death and grief 163

Pandemic 164, 174, 179

Personality as a house 176

Pieces of Mind Exhibit 42, 148

Pictures with shards of glass (Adobe Stock overlay) to represent decompensation 43

Questions—Could a patient's photography predict health and strength? 59

Relationship of Photography to Schizophrenia 43, 137-142

Thinking errors, resentment replaced with creativity 153, 168-169

Walking the Talk 11

You win when. . . 15-16

Made in the USA
Columbia, SC
20 August 2024

0e122bb5-19f4-490e-9932-350b92dc7797R01